EPIC LEGO® ADVENTURES

with Bricks You Already Have

Build Crazy Worlds Where Aliens Live on the Moon, Dinosaurs Walk Among Us,
Scientists Battle Mutant Bugs and You Bring Their Hilarious Tales to Life

SARAH DEES

Author of *Awesome LEGO® Creations with Bricks
You Already Have* and Founder of Frugal Fun for Boys and Girls

PAGE STREET
PUBLISHING CO.

DEDICATION

To Jordan and to our little LEGO builders—Aidan, Gresham, Owen, Jonathan and Janie.
You all love a good laugh, and I couldn't have created this book with anyone else!

PAGE STREET
PUBLISHING CO.

As a member of 1% for the Planet, Page Street Publishing protects our planet by donating to nonprofits like The Trustees, which focuses on local land conservation. Learn more at onepercentfortheplanet.org.

CONTENTS

HOW TO USE THIS BOOK

EPIC ADVENTURES . . . WITH LEGO!

Hello, LEGO fan! If you're holding this book, chances are that LEGO bricks and minifigures are already some of your favorite things. Now it's time to turn those bricks into crazy and hilarious adventures! This book will take you on five epic LEGO adventures, and you'll be laughing all the way.

The great thing about this book is that it's not just an adventure book. It's also an instruction book! In the pages to follow, you'll find parts lists and step-by-step instructions for all of the LEGO projects shown in the stories because it can be a real bummer to see an awesome idea and then not be able to figure out what pieces were used to build it. Use the parts list to organize your bricks before building or to figure out which pieces you need. Follow the step-by-step instructions for easy building. We've got you covered with everything you need to know to assemble the LEGO creations you see here!

We don't want you to worry if you don't have the exact bricks shown in this book. The stories and the project ideas are meant to be a springboard for your own imagination. Don't feel limited by the colors and bricks that we chose! If you don't have all of the bricks needed, then get creative with the bricks you have. If you want to change a project, then go for it!

ORDERING INDIVIDUAL BRICKS

You may see a project, however, that you want to build exactly as it's shown in the book. Luckily, it's not very difficult to order the individual bricks you need to complete a project! There are basically two options for ordering bricks, and both will require help from your parents. One is to order from the Pick-A-Brick section on www.Lego.com, and the other is to order from a third party LEGO seller. You might not be aware of this, but every LEGO brick has a tiny ID number on it, usually on the underside. This ID number is specific to that part, but not specific to the color. So if you put that number in the search bar on the Pick-A-Brick site, you will be able to see all of the colors available for that brick. Then you can order the one you want. However, note that orders from Pick-A-Brick can take a few weeks to arrive.

Another option is to order from www.bricklink.com. Brick Link is a site that hosts many different sellers of LEGO bricks, and you can purchase new and used bricks as well as unopened sets and custom sets. The prices on Brick Link are related to supply and demand, meaning that a basic brick in a common color will cost only a few cents, while a hard-to-find collectible minifigure will sell for much more. Each vendor on Brick Link charges for shipping separately, so be aware of this when adding bricks to your cart. If you buy five different parts from five different vendors, you are going to pay five different shipping fees! Look for a vendor with a large inventory, and try to find one person who has several things that you need.

LEGO bricks come in many different colors, many more colors than what was available when I was a kid! The colors are listed on the Pick-A-Brick section of Lego.com, and the Brick Link site also has a color guide. Because Brick Link vendors sell both new and used LEGO bricks, they have a system of color names that includes older colors which have now been discontinued. The Brick Link color system names are used in this book. Please note, however, that the bricks called light gray and dark gray are called light bluish gray and dark bluish gray on Brick Link.

Be sure to get permission from Mom or Dad before making any purchases, and get their help when using websites like Brick Link and the official LEGO site!

BRICK GUIDE

The projects in this book make use of many different LEGO bricks! Did you know that LEGO bricks have names? If you buy a set, you don't need to know the names of the pieces in order to build the set. But what happens if you want to order individual bricks online? In this brick guide, you will find the names of many of the bricks that we have used in this book. This is not an exhaustive list of all of the LEGO bricks available, but this guide will help you to understand the terms used in the parts lists for each project and to find individual bricks when ordering online.

There are differences in the names of bricks depending on whether you are ordering from Lego.com's Pick-A-Brick site or from a third party LEGO vendor such as Brick Link (www.bricklink.com). Throughout the book, the Brick Link names are primarily used since it is an easier site to order from.

Remember that any LEGO brick can be easily located on either Pick-A-Brick (www.lego.com) or Brick Link by searching the ID number on the brick. This tiny number is usually located on the underside of the brick.

BRICKS

These are bricks. Count the number of dots (studs) to determine the brick's size. For example, the green brick is a 2 x 4 brick, the yellow brick is a 2 x 6 and the blue brick is a 2 x 3.

MODIFIED BRICKS

These are bricks that are modified in some way. Pick-A-Brick calls them "bricks, special," and Brick Link calls them "bricks, modified." Bricks can be modified with a handle, a pin, a clip, extra studs and more. The green brick is a headlight. Notice that there is a small notch in the bottom front of the brick. There are also 1 x 1 bricks with a stud on the side that do not have the notch. In this book, the parts lists specify between the two types.

ROUND BRICKS

The brown brick is a 4 x 4 round brick, the red is a 2 x 2, and the smallest ones are 1 x 1. The yellow brick is a 2 x 2 dome, which is grouped with the round bricks on Brick Link.

PLATES

Both Pick-A-Brick and Brick Link use the word plates for these flat bricks. The dark red brick is a 4 x 4 round plate. The black brick is a wedge plate. If the sides are equal on a wedge plate, then it is just called a wedge plate. The black brick is a 3 x 8 wedge plate right, because this shape has a right or left orientation.

MODIFIED PLATES

Like bricks, plates can also be modified with a handle, a clip, a tooth, claws, etc. These bricks are called "plates, special" on Pick-A-Brick and "plates, modified" on Brick Link. The brown brick is a 1 x 2 hinge plate with two fingers, locking. This means that it connects with the dark gray brick in this picture to create a hinge that can be bent but that doesn't move freely.

Here are a few more of the modified plates used in this book. From left to right they are a 1 x 2 plate with a ball on the side, a 2 x 2 turntable, a 1 x 2—1 x 2 hinge and a 1 x 2 plate with a socket on the end (top of the photo). The ball and socket plates work together to create a moveable joint.

SLOPE BRICKS

These are slope bricks. They are organized under "slope" on Brick Link and "bricks, sloping" on Pick-A-Brick. However, Pick-A-Brick refers to bricks such as the orange brick and the dark blue brick as roof tiles. The 2 x 2 lime green brick is an inverted slope. The dark gray brick is a 1 x 2 slope, 30 degree. The brown brick is a 1 x 1 slope, 30 degree. The red brick is a 1 x 4 curved slope.

BRACKETS

These bricks are called brackets (Brick Link) or angle plates (Pick-A-Brick). Brackets are very useful for building on the side. Either site refers to the size of a bracket in two parts with measurements given for each side. For example, the light gray bracket is a 1 x 2—2 x 2 and the blue bracket is a 1 x 2—1 x 4. The green bracket is inverted since the second side goes upward instead of down.

TILES

Plate bricks that are smooth on top are called tiles. Pick-A-Brick refers to them as flat tiles, while on Brick Link they are tiles. Some tiles are decorated with pictures such as maps or gauges or smart phone apps.

TECHNIC BRICKS

The bricks shown in this photo are referred to as Technic bricks even though they also come in many sets that are not Technic sets. Bricks with holes are Technic bricks. Technic axles are X-shaped and are measured by the number of studs long. There are several types of Technic pins that can be used for a variety of functions.

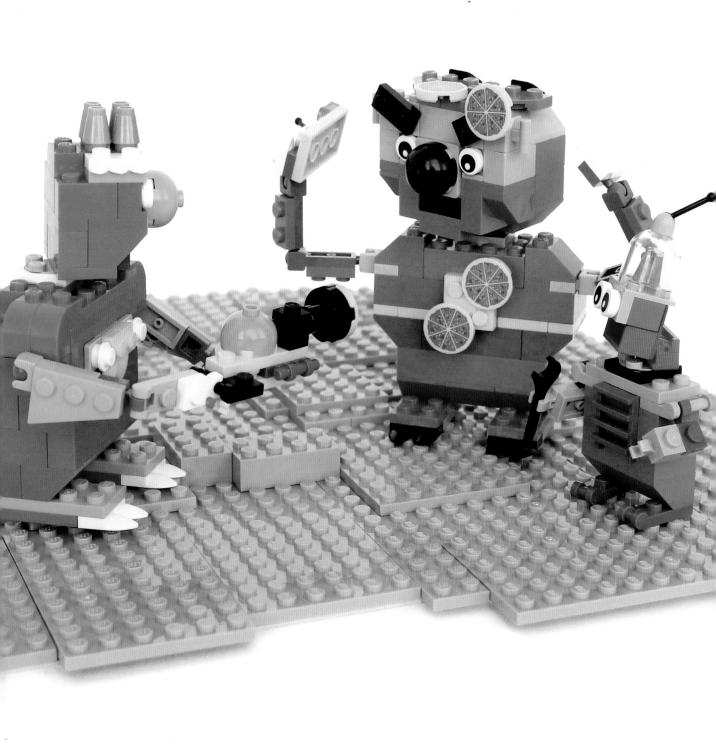

CRASH LANDING ON THE MOON

Build an outer space encounter between astronauts and aliens! Let your imagination come to life with crazy aliens who are constantly fixing their malfunctioning space blaster. Then add astronauts! The warning light flashes on the spaceship, and the astronaut is forced to land on the moon. Unfortunately, his split-second decision is too late and his ship crashes. Frantically, he calls for help on his radio. More astronauts arrive to help him, and who should they encounter but some mischievous aliens wielding a space blaster that shoots something no one was expecting!

THE FAR SIDE OF THE MOON

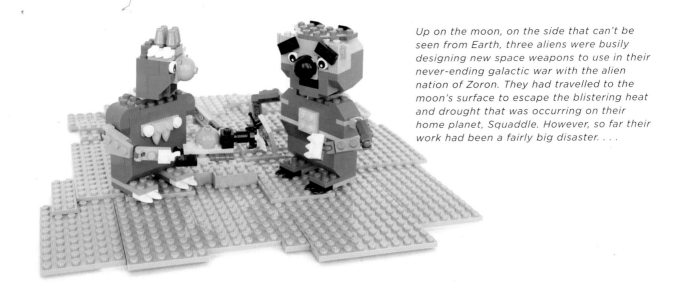

Up on the moon, on the side that can't be seen from Earth, three aliens were busily designing new space weapons to use in their never-ending galactic war with the alien nation of Zoron. They had travelled to the moon's surface to escape the blistering heat and drought that was occurring on their home planet, Squaddle. However, so far their work had been a fairly big disaster. . . .

"Glump, the space blaster is malfunctioning again. When I push the button, nothing happens. I can't get it to shoot at all!"

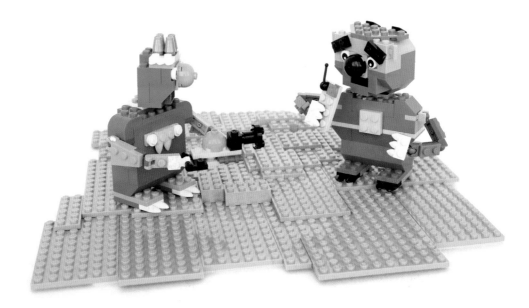

"Not again!" Glump groaned. "I'll get Gadget to fix it."

Glump yelled into his radio. "GADGET! Get over here and take a look at this space blaster!"

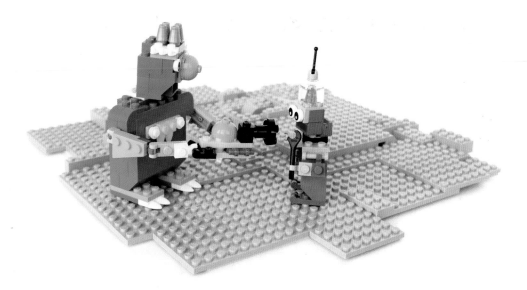

Gadget grabbed some tools and began working on the blaster. "Grooby, I think the space blaster is fixed now!" Gadget squeaked. "I replaced the release button, but I can't find anything else wrong with it."

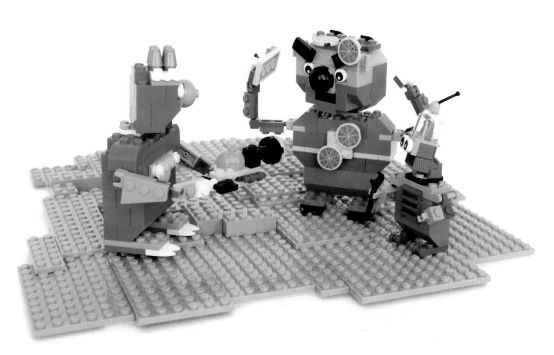

"On second thought, maybe there IS something else wrong with it!" said Gadget, as a torrent of pizzas shot out of the blaster and hit Glump directly in the face. Glump wiped the cheese off his forehead and then exploded in frustration.

"GADGET!" hollered Glump. "Give me that screwdriver! Next time, I'm fixing this myself!"

GROOBY THE HAPPY ALIEN

Grooby the alien is goofy and a little absentminded. For some reason, he is always the one to operate the space blaster even though he is probably not the smartest choice! His open mouth gives him a humorous expression. Pretend that Grooby is shooting pizzas all over the place, or pretend that his space blaster shoots slime or space dust or anything you can imagine!

PARTS LIST

GREEN BRICKS
3—2 x 4 bricks
3—2 x 3 bricks
4—2 x 2 bricks
4—1 x 4 bricks
6—1 x 2 bricks
4—1 x 1 bricks
2—1 x 1 bricks with a stud on the side (headlight)
3—2 x 2 slopes, inverted
3—2 x 4 plates
2—1 x 4 plates
4—2 x 3 plates
1—2 x 2 plate
6—1 x 2 plates
2—1 x 2 slopes, inverted
1—1 x 2—1 x 2 bracket, inverted
4—1 x 2 x 1⅓ bricks modified with a curved top

LIME GREEN BRICKS
1—2 x 2 round brick with dome top
2—2 x 4 plates
2—1 x 2 plates
1—1 x 2—2 x 2 bracket, inverted
1—2 x 3 wedge plate, right
1—2 x 3 wedge plate, left

GRAY BRICKS
2—1 x 2 light gray plates with a handle on the end
2—1 x 2 light gray plates with a socket on the end
1—1 x 4—1 x 2 light gray bracket
2—1 x 2 dark gray plates with a ball on the side
2—1 x 1 dark gray plates with clips, horizontal

ASSORTED BRICKS
4—1 x 1 white plates with one claw
2—1 x 2 white plates with three claws

2—1 x 1 white plates with clips
2—1 x 1 white round plates
1—2 x 2 turntable plate white/gray
4—1 x 1 gold cones
1—1 x 2 x 1 magenta panel with two sides
2—1 x 1 light orange plates with one claw
2—eyes

SPACE GUN
2—1 x 4 yellow plates
1—2 x 2 orange round brick with dome top
1—2 x 2 black round plate
1—1 x 2 black plate with a handle on the side
1—1 x 1 black round brick
1—1 x 1 black brick with a stud on the side
1—1 x 1 lime green round plate
1—1 x 2 dark gray plate with a handle on the side, open ends

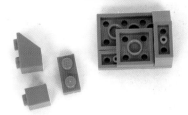

STEP 1: Start with the alien's head. Find a 2 x 4 green plate, a 2 x 2 green plate and a 1 x 4 green plate.

STEP 2: Attach the two larger plates with the 2 x 2 plate as shown.

STEP 3: Add a 1 x 2 inverted slope, a 1 x 1 brick and a 1 x 2 plate on each side of the underside of the face.

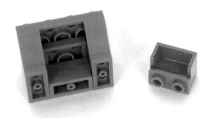

STEP 4: Find a 1 x 2—1 x 2 inverted bracket, a 1 x 2 green brick and a 1 x 2 x 1 magenta panel. If you don't have the panel in the magenta color, use another color.

STEP 5: Attach the 1 x 2 green brick to the underside of the head, and attach the other two bricks as shown.

STEP 6: Attach the mouth to the alien's head.

STEP 7: Find a lime green 1 x 2—2 x 2 bracket (inverted) and a 2 x 2 dome brick.

STEP 8: Attach the bracket under the green plate as shown, and then add the dome brick.

STEP 9: Add a 2 x 3 green brick, two 1 x 2 green bricks, two 1 x 1 green bricks with a stud on the side (headlight) and two eyes to the head.

STEP 10: Place two 2 x 3 green plates on the top of the alien's head. Then add four 1 x 1 gold cones, two 1 x 2 lime green plates and two 1 x 2 white plates with claws as decoration on his head. If you don't have those bricks, use something else!

STEP 11: Build the alien's body. Start with three 2 x 2 green inverted slopes, one 1 x 2 green brick and one 1 x 4 green brick.

STEP 12: Add a layer of green bricks to the body.

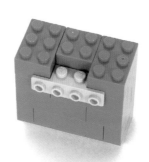

STEP 13: Build two more layers on the alien's body. Bricks shown are two 2 x 4 bricks, two 2 x 2 bricks, two 1 x 4 bricks and two 1 x 2 bricks.

STEP 14: Place a 1 x 4—1 x 2 light gray bracket on the body. Then add two 2 x 3 green bricks and a 2 x 2 green brick.

STEP 15: Add two 1 x 2 green plates on top of the gray bracket. Then gather the bricks shown.

STEP 16: Build the alien's shoulders and neck as shown. The turntable brick is sitting on top of two 2 x 4 green plates.

STEP 17: Place one 1 x 2 dark gray plate with a ball on the side under each set of curved bricks. Add a 1 x 2 green plate on the top of each shoulder.

STEP 18: Add two 1 x 1 light orange plates with a claw and two 1 x 1 white round plates to the front of the alien for decoration. Or substitute other bricks that you have on hand.

STEP 19: Assemble the alien's arms as shown.

STEP 20: Build the alien's feet. Each foot is one 2 x 4 lime green plate, one 2 x 3 green plate and two 1 x 1 white plates with one claw.

STEP 21: Attach the arms, feet and head to the alien's body, and the alien is complete!

STEP 22: Build the space blaster gun. Gather the pieces shown.

STEP 23: Attach the 1 x 2 black plate with a handle, 1 x 1 lime green round plate and 1 x 2 dark gray plate with a handle (open ends) to the 1 x 4 yellow plate.

STEP 24: Add the other 1 x 4 yellow plate, the orange dome and the 1 x 1 black brick with a stud on the side as shown.

STEP 25: Complete the gun by adding a 1 x 1 black round brick and a 2 x 2 black round plate.

Now find something for your alien to shoot with his space blaster! If you don't have pizzas, use 1 x 1 round plates in translucent colors to be slime, or shoot gray bricks to be moon dust. Or think of your own ideas!

GLUMP THE ANGRY ALIEN

Glump the alien is certainly not the most patient guy you've ever met! Change his face from serious to angry by adjusting the tilt of his eyebrows. Fully posable arms make him a lot of fun for creating hilarious scenes. Put his hands on his hips, or make him raise his fist when he is arguing with Grooby and Gadget about the silly space blaster repairs!

PARTS LIST

BLUE BRICKS
3—2 x 6 bricks
3—2 x 4 bricks
1—1 x 4 brick
2—1 x 6 bricks
1—1 x 8 brick
1—2 x 2 brick
2—2 x 2 slopes
5—2 x 2 slopes, inverted
2—1 x 2 slopes, inverted
4—2 x 4 plates
1—2 x 6 plate
1—2 x 2 plate
12—1 x 2 plates
2—3 x 3 wedge plates, cut corner

LIGHT GRAY BRICKS
1—2 x 4 brick
2—1 x 2 bricks

2—2 x 2 slopes
2—1 x 2 slopes
2—1 x 1 bricks with a stud on the side, headlight
2—1 x 1 bricks with a stud on the side
2—2 x 3 plates
1—2 x 2 plate
2—1 x 2 plates with a socket on the side
1—bracket 1 x 2—2 x 2
1—bracket 1 x 2—2 x 2, inverted
2—1 x 1 bricks with handle

DARK GRAY BRICKS
1—2 x 4 brick
1—1 x 4 brick
2—2 x 2 slopes, inverted
2—1 x 2 slopes, inverted
4—1 x 2 plates with a socket and a ball on the ends
2—1 x 2 plates with a ball on the side

BLACK BRICKS
2—1 x 2 plates
2—1 x 1 slopes, 30 degree
1—1 x 2 slope, 30 degree
1—2 x 2 dome
4—1 x 1 plates with one claw
1—turntable, 2 x 2 plate

ASSORTED BRICKS
2—2 x 3 yellow plates
2—2 x 2 yellow plates
2—1 x 3 yellow plates
2—eyes
2—1 x 2 white plates with three claws
1—2 x 4 tan plate
1—antenna
1—1 x 1 translucent orange plate

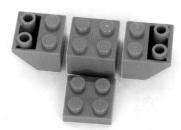

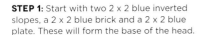

STEP 1: Start with two 2 x 2 blue inverted slopes, a 2 x 2 blue brick and a 2 x 2 blue plate. These will form the base of the head.

STEP 2: Add a 2 x 6 blue brick, a 2 x 4 blue plate and a 1 x 2 slope (30 degree).

STEP 3: Add four 1 x 2 blue plates next to the black 1 x 2 slope, two on each side.

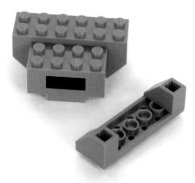

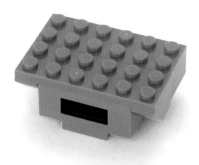

STEP 4: Place a 2 x 4 blue plate above the alien's mouth. Then attach two 1 x 2 blue inverted slopes to the underside of a 2 x 6 blue plate.

STEP 5: Attach the 2 x 6 plate to the front of the face. Note that the two sections of the head are still not attached to each other.

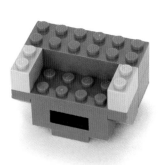

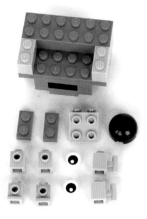

STEP 6: Add two 1 x 2 light gray bricks and a 2 x 6 blue brick to the head.

STEP 7: Gather the bricks shown for building the alien's face.

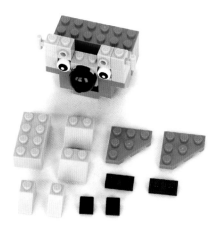

STEP 8: Stack the two 1 x 2 blue plates and place them in the middle of the face. Then add a 1 x 1 brick with a stud on the side (headlight style) and a 1 x 1 brick with a stud on the side on each side of the face.

STEP 9: Attach the light gray bracket on top of the two 1 x 2 blue plates. Then add the eyes, the two bricks with a handle on the side and the 2 x 2 dome brick as a nose. Then gather the bricks shown.

STEP 10: Fill in the top of the head with the light gray bricks shown.

STEP 11: Add the two blue wedge plates and the two 1 x 1 black slopes to the top of the head.

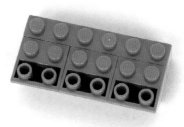

STEP 12: Attach the 1 x 2 black plates to the bricks with a stud on the side to make the eyebrows.

STEP 13: Build the body. Start with three 2 x 2 blue inverted slope bricks and a 1 x 6 blue brick.

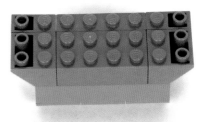

STEP 14: Add a 1 x 6 blue brick and a 2 x 6 blue brick.

STEP 15: Build another layer with two 2 x 2 dark gray inverted slopes, two 1 x 2 dark gray inverted slopes, a 1 x 4 dark gray brick and a 2 x 4 dark gray brick.

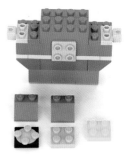

STEP 16: Use yellow plates to create the alien's belt. Place a 1 x 2—2 x 2 bracket (inverted) in the middle. The bracket sits on top of the gray brick with no yellow plate under it.

STEP 17: Build another layer with two 2 x 4 blue bricks and a 1 x 8 blue brick. Or fill in the space with a different combination of blue bricks.

STEP 18: Add two 1 x 2 light gray plates with a socket, two 1 x 2 blue plates, a 2 x 4 blue brick and a 1 x 4 blue brick. Then gather the bricks shown.

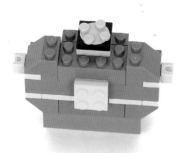

STEP 19: Place the slope bricks on the shoulders as shown. Then stack the 2 x 2 light gray plate and the 2 x 2 turntable. These will be the alien's neck and allow the head to turn. Place the 2 x 2 yellow plate on the light gray bracket.

STEP 20: Assemble the alien's arms as shown.

STEP 21: Build the feet. Each foot has a 2 x 4 blue plate, a 2 x 3 light gray plate and two 1 x 1 black plates with a claw.

STEP 22: Attach the head, arms and feet to the alien's body.

You can make your alien look angry by adjusting the eyebrows and posing his arms. Build him a walkie-talkie using a 2 x 4 tan plate, an antenna and a 1 x 1 translucent orange plate. Now he's ready to play! Pretend that your aliens are building a new space blaster. Or create a spaceship for them to ride in.

GADGET THE HELPFUL ALIEN

Gadget the alien makes anyone smile as soon as they see him! His head rotates and tilts which almost seems to make him come alive. Give Gadget tools to use as he fixes the space blaster that's always breaking, or pretend that he is zooming through space with his friends Glump and Grooby on his alien space cruiser (page 35).

PARTS LIST

BLUE BRICKS
2—2 x 4 bricks
2—2 x 2 slopes, inverted
1—1 x 2 brick

LIGHT GRAY BRICKS
1—2 x 4 plate
2—1 x 2 plates with a handle on the side

1—1 x 2—2 x 2 bracket
1—1 x 2 plate
2—1 x 1 plates
2—1 x 2 plates with a clip on the end, horizontal

DARK GRAY BRICKS
2—1 x 2 plates with a handle on the end
2—1 x 1 plates with clips, horizontal
1—1 x 2 plate modified with a ladder

ASSORTED BRICKS
1—red hinge brick, 1 x 2 base
1—2 x 2 red hinge brick top plate thin
1—1 x 1 translucent orange cone
1—2 x 2 turntable plate, black/gray
2—eyes
1—1 x 2 x 1 magenta panel with two sides
1—2 x 2 x 1⅔ clear dome, hollow
1—antenna

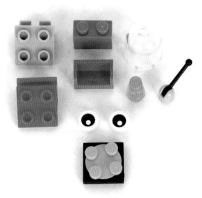

STEP 1: Gather the pieces needed to build Gadget's head.

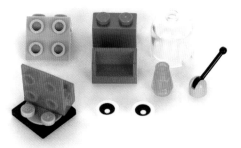

STEP 2: Attach the top plate to the hinge brick. Then attach this to the turntable.

STEP 3: Attach the 1 x 2 blue brick and the magenta panel to the hinge brick.

STEP 4: Add the light gray bracket and the eyes to the alien's head.

STEP 5: Complete the head by adding the orange cone, the clear dome and the antenna.

STEP 6: Start on Gadget's body by finding two 2 x 2 inverted slope bricks.

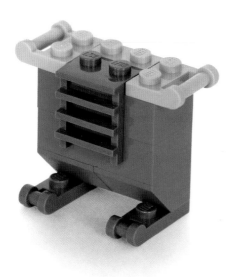

STEP 7: The body is simple to build. Add two 2 x 4 blue bricks. Then add a 1 x 2 light gray plate, two 1 x 2 light gray plates with handles and the 1 x 2 dark gray plate with a ladder. Use 1 x 2 dark gray plates with a handle on the end as feet.

STEP 8: Add a 2 x 4 light gray plate to the top of the alien's body.

STEP 9: Assemble the arms as shown. Then attach them to the handles on each shoulder.

STEP 10: Attach the head to the body, and Gadget the alien is complete! Build Gadget's space cruiser (directions on page 35), or design your own vehicle for him to drive. Or pretend that he is "fixing" a space vehicle or a space blaster gun and now it does something crazy!

CRASH LANDING!

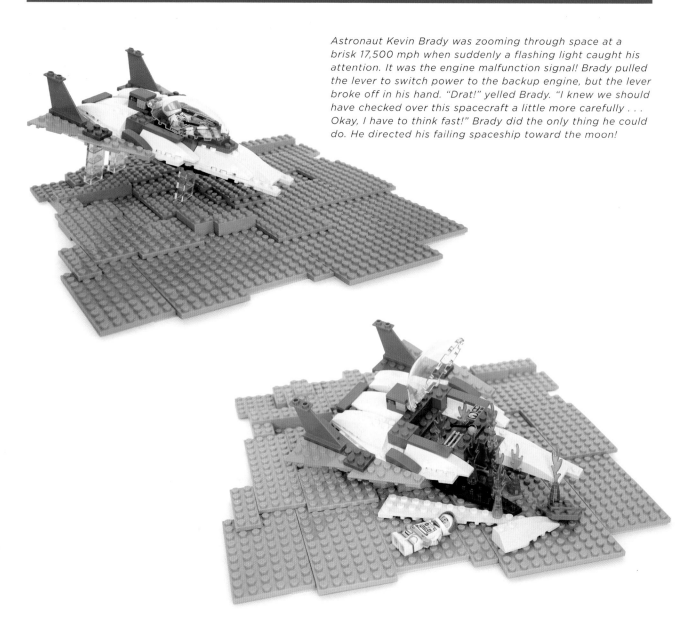

Astronaut Kevin Brady was zooming through space at a brisk 17,500 mph when suddenly a flashing light caught his attention. It was the engine malfunction signal! Brady pulled the lever to switch power to the backup engine, but the lever broke off in his hand. "Drat!" yelled Brady. "I knew we should have checked over this spacecraft a little more carefully . . . Okay, I have to think fast!" Brady did the only thing he could do. He directed his failing spaceship toward the moon!

Unfortunately, Brady's split-second decision was a moment too late. Unable to adequately slow down the ship before landing, Brady crashed into the surface of the moon. Instantly the front end of the ship went up in flames! "Aaaarrrghhh!" yelled Brady as he was launched from the spaceship and then skidded to a stop on the surface of the moon.

"Yow!" he groaned. "These space suits do NOT have enough padding!"

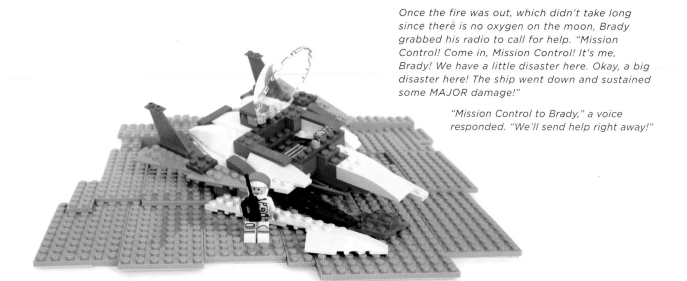

Once the fire was out, which didn't take long since there is no oxygen on the moon, Brady grabbed his radio to call for help. "Mission Control! Come in, Mission Control! It's me, Brady! We have a little disaster here. Okay, a big disaster here! The ship went down and sustained some MAJOR damage!"

"Mission Control to Brady," a voice responded. "We'll send help right away!"

"Boy, am I glad to see you guys!" Brady said to Tucker and Luke, the astronauts who had arrived to help. "Let's get this spaceship back in working order!"

ASTROTEK 3.0 SPACESHIP

Astronaut Brady will love the speed and power of this nimble spacecraft as he zooms through space on his mission to the moon! This spaceship is equipped with a sleek design, an opening cockpit and three rocket engines on the back. If you don't have the exact pieces shown, adapt the spaceship with the parts you have.

PARTS LIST

WHITE BRICKS
4—1 x 6 curved slopes
1—3 x 12 wedge plate, right
1—3 x 12 wedge plate, left
1—3 x 8 wedge plate, right
1—3 x 8 wedge plate, left
1—6 x 12 wedge plate, right
1—6 x 12 wedge plate, left
4—6 x 2 wedges, right
4—6 x 2 wedges, left

LIGHT GRAY BRICKS
1—6 x 10 plate
1—2 x 8 brick
2—1 x 6 bricks
2—1 x 3 bricks
1—2 x 6 plate
1—1 x 2 plate
1—1 x 2 plate with clips on the side
3—wheels with pin hole
1—3 x 6 wedge plate, right

1—3 x 6 wedge plate, left
1—6 x 4 inverted curved wedge
3—2 x 2 plates with pin hole

DARK GRAY BRICKS
1—4 x 8 plate
3—2 x 6 plates
1—2 x 4 plate
2—2 x 2 plates
1—1 x 6 plate
1—1 x 4 brick

BLUE BRICKS
1—2 x 8 plate
1—2 x 6 plate
2—2 x 2 plates
2—1 x 2 plates
1—2 x 2 tile
3—1 x 4 tiles
2—3 x 1 curved slopes
5—2 x 2 bricks
1—3 x 6 wedge plate, right
1—3 x 6 wedge plate, left

1—3 x 4 wedge plate
2—tails 4 x 3 x 1

ASSORTED BRICKS
1—8 x 6 x 2⅓ bubble canopy with
   handle, clear
2—3 x 8 dark blue wedge plates, right
2—3 x 8 dark blue wedge plates, left
4—2 x 2 black plates
1—1 x 2 black plate
3—black pins
1—1 x 2 translucent blue plate
1—3 x 6 orange wedge plate, right
1—3 x 6 orange wedge plate, left
1—1 x 2 orange plate
1—1 x 2 tile with gauges
1—1 x 2 silver grill
1—antenna
11—1 x 2 clear bricks
1 x 1 orange cones
Fire bricks

STEP 1: Start with a light gray 6 x 4 inverted curved wedge and the light gray bricks shown.

STEP 2: Add a 6 x 10 light gray plate, a 2 x 6 blue plate and two 3 x 8 dark blue wedge plates. There will be space between the blue plate and the curved wedge on the bottom.

STEP 3: Add two 3 x 12 white wedge plates, two more dark blue 3 x 8 wedge plates, a 2 x 4 dark gray plate and a 2 x 8 blue plate. The two sections of the ship are still not attached.

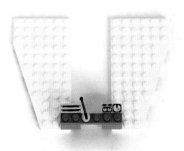

STEP 4: Attach the two sections with a 4 x 8 dark gray plate, two 2 x 6 dark gray plates and a 1 x 4 blue tile.

STEP 5: Find two 6 x 12 white wedge plates. These will form the base for the wings.

STEP 6: Start building the cockpit with two 2 x 2 blue bricks, a 1 x 6 dark gray plate, a 1 x 2 grill and a 1 x 2 tile with gauges. Add an antenna to the dark gray plate.

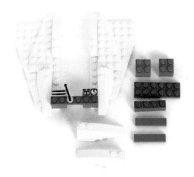

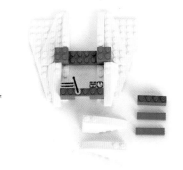

STEP 7: On each side, attach a 6 x 2 wedge, a 1 x 6 curved slope and a 3 x 8 wedge plate.

STEP 8: Gather the bricks shown.

STEP 9: Place the 2 x 6 dark gray plate and two 2 x 2 blue bricks across the wings as shown.

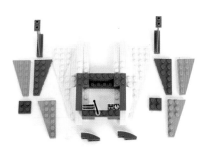

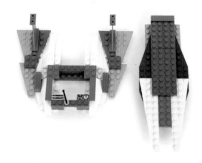

STEP 10: Place the two 6 x 2 wedge bricks next to the 1 x 6 curved slopes. Add the 1 x 4 dark gray brick and the two 1 x 4 tiles. Then gather the bricks shown for each wing.

STEP 11: Assemble the wings as shown. Add one 1 x 3 blue curved slope on each side of the cockpit.

STEP 12: Your two completed sections of the spaceship should now look like this.

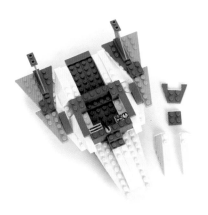

STEP 13: Attach the two sections as shown. The base section should stick out past the wing section by one row of studs on the back end.

STEP 14: Add two 1 x 6 white curved slopes, a 2 x 2 blue brick and a 1 x 2 blue plate in front of the cockpit. Find two more 2 x 6 white wedges, a 2 x 2 blue plate and a 3 x 4 blue wedge plate.

STEP 15: Use these bricks to fill in the front of the spaceship as shown.

STEP 16: Gather the bricks shown for the cockpit windscreen.

STEP 17: Stack the 1 x 2 light gray plate with clips on top of the 1 x 2 orange plate. Place the 1 x 2 translucent blue plate on top of the 1 x 2 blue plate.

STEP 18: Place both of these on top of the 2 x 2 blue plate.

STEP 19: Attach the stacked bricks to the two 2 x 6 white wedge bricks as shown. Attach the windscreen to the clips and then add the 2 x 2 blue tile.

STEP 20: Attach the windscreen to the body of the spaceship as shown.

STEP 21: Gather the pieces shown for building the engines. You will need three wheels that have a pin hole, four 2 x 2 black plates, one 1 x 2 black plate, one 1 x 2 light gray plate, three black pins and three 2 x 2 light gray plates modified with a pin hole.

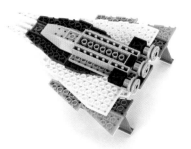

STEP 22: Assemble the engines as shown.

STEP 23: Add the engines to the bottom of the spaceship.

STEP 24: Cover the engines with a 2 x 6 light gray plate, and the spaceship is complete!

Now your LEGO astronaut is ready to zoom off on an adventure in outer space! Be sure to pack him an oxygen tank and some tools for repairing his spaceship, just in case.

Build a crash scene by removing bricks from the front end. Create an engine fire by using 1 x 1 translucent orange cones and fire bricks. You can prop the spaceship up at an angle by attaching 1 x 2 clear bricks on one side under the ship.

PIZZA BLASTER

Once the spaceship had been repaired, Brady and the other astronauts decided they would collect some samples of moon rock and conduct some other experiments before heading back to Earth. They rumbled over the surface of the moon in their rugged moon rover until they found a good place to dig. Tucker grabbed a shovel and started collecting moon rock.

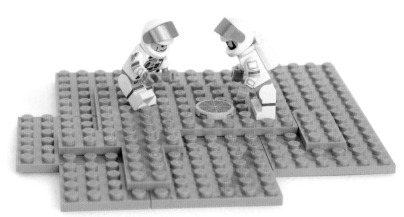

One puzzling discovery was a pizza that Brady and Luke found sitting right on the surface of the moon! "This is extremely bizarre," said Luke.

"You're right," said Brady. "Let's get back to Tucker and see what he thinks."

"Wow, you guys ordered pizza up here on the moon?" said Tucker.

"What? No! We just found this! Isn't that a little odd?" asked Brady.

"No, that just confirms it!" Tucker replied.

"Confirms WHAT?" said Luke.

"That the moon is made out of cheese!"

"Tucker, you dummy, even if it is, and I'm not saying it really is, it's made out of cheese! Not cheese PIZZA! Who in the world could have made this pizza?" Luke exclaimed.

"I don't know," said Tucker. "It's not like there are any aliens around here. Well, I'm starving. Let's eat!"

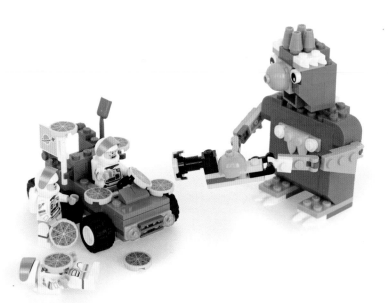

Suddenly the astronauts found themselves face to face with a giant green . . . thing! What WAS this bizarre creature?

"Tucker," Luke yelled, "you just said there aren't any aliens here! So what is this? The Easter Bunny?"

But Tucker didn't have time to answer because the big green thing that was obviously an alien blasted them all with pizzas! "Take that, you trespassers!" he yelled. "You're surrounded!"

"AHHHHHH," screamed the astronauts at a volume that could probably be heard all the way back on Earth. "Step on the gas!" yelled Luke, and Tucker did! He zoomed away from the big green alien with pizzas still clinging to the sides of the moon rover.

Tucker was driving so rapidly that he didn't see Gadget aboard his space cruiser, and he crashed right into Gadget! The astronauts heard a terrible crunch as the moon rover lost a wheel and Luke was thrown from the vehicle.

"Oh!" squeaked Gadget. "I've been hit by some strange little creatures! What are you? Where are you going? What is that thing you're driving? Do you need me to repair that? I'll get my tools!"

All Tucker could manage to say was, "Um . . . okay?"

MOON ROVER

Astronauts can easily explore the surface of the moon with this nimble moon rover. Its rugged tires can rumble over rocks and drive through valleys, and it also has plenty of speed so that the astronauts can flee from aliens. Equip your moon rover with a shovel and tools for collecting samples of moon rock. There is room in the back for two astronauts to ride.

PARTS LIST

BLUE BRICKS
2—2 x 4 plates
3—1 x 4 plates
2—1 x 2 plates
1—1 x 4 tile
1—1 x 2 brick
4—1 x 4 bricks
2—1 x 1 slopes, 30 degree

LIGHT GRAY BRICKS
1—1 x 2–1 x 4 bracket
1—1 x 2 plate
1—1 x 2 x 1 panel
1—1 x 1 brick with a stud on the side
6—2 x 2 plates with one axle

DARK GRAY BRICKS
1—4 x 10 dark gray plate
1—1 x 4 plate
1—1 x 2 brick

1—1 x 2 grill
1—1 x 2 brick modified with a clip
2—1 x 1 bricks modified with clips
1—1 x 1 plate with a clip, horizontal
1—1 x 1 plate with a clip light

ASSORTED BRICKS
6—wheels
1—steering wheel
2—1 x 1 round plates, translucent yellow
Assorted tools, flag

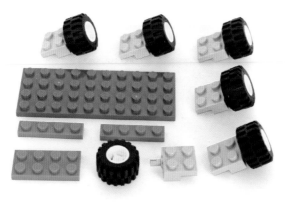

STEP 1: Gather the pieces shown for building the base of the moon rover.

STEP 2: Attach the wheels and the blue plates to the underside of the 4 x 10 dark gray plate.

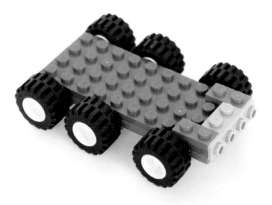

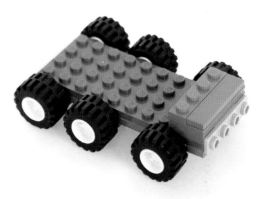

STEP 3: Add a light gray bracket and two 1 x 2 blue plates to the front of the moon rover.

STEP 4: Add a 2 x 4 blue plate, a 1 x 4 blue plate and a 1 x 4 blue tile to the front.

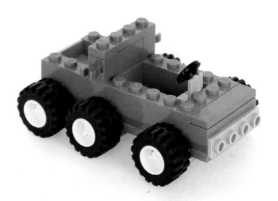

STEP 5: Add blue bricks and a 1 x 2 x 1 light gray panel as shown. Place a 1 x 2 light gray plate under the steering wheel to raise it up a little. Add the steering wheel to the vehicle.

STEP 6: Build the center bar with a 1 x 2 dark gray brick, two 1 x 1 dark gray bricks with a clip and a 1 x 4 dark gray plate.

STEP 7: Gather the bricks shown for adding details to the moon rover. Attach a 1 x 1 dark gray plate with a clip to a 1 x 1 light gray brick with a stud on the side. Attach 1 x 1 slopes, a 1 x 2 grill and 1 x 1 yellow round plates to complete the front.

STEP 8: Add the bricks with clips to the back of the moon rover. Then find some tools to attach to the clips, as well as a space flag.

The moon rover is now complete and ready for the astronauts to use as they explore the moon's surface!

The astronauts can grab a shovel from the moon rover and scoop up some moon rock samples. Well, at least until the aliens find them! Try creating a crash scene with the moon rover and Gadget's space cruiser. Remove some bricks such as the front wheels and the headlights to create the crash.

ALIEN SPACE CRUISER

Gadget the alien loves to zoom around space in this awesome space cruiser! Since he loves to fix things, he doesn't even mind when someone crashes into him! This cruiser combines some of the design elements of a car such as a front grill with imaginative elements to create a fun space craft. Clear bricks underneath the cruiser give the appearance that the cruiser is hovering.

PARTS LIST

DARK GRAY BRICKS
1—4 x 10 plate
1—2 x 8 plate
2—1 x 6 plates
1—2 x 4 plate
2—2 x 2 plates
1—1 x 4 plate
3—1 x 2 plates
1—3 x 6 wedge plate, right
1—3 x 6 wedge plate, left
2—1 x 2 slopes, inverted
2—2 x 2 slopes, two bricks high
2—1 x 2 bricks, two bricks high
1—1 x 2—2 x 2 bracket

2—1 x 2 grills
1—1 x 2 plate with two handles
2—binoculars

LIGHT GRAY BRICKS
1—4 x 12 plate
1—4 x 10 plate
5—2 x 4 bricks
2—2 x 2 bricks
1—1 x 8 brick
1—2 x 4 slope
2—6 x 2 wedges, inverted right
2—6 x 2 wedges, inverted left
1—10 x 3 wedge, right
1—10 x 3 wedge, left

ASSORTED BRICKS
1—3 x 8 purple wedge plate, right
1—3 x 8 purple wedge plate, left
1—2 x 4 black wedge, triple right
1—2 x 4 black wedge, triple left
1—1 x 4 black plate
4—1 x 2 clear bricks
1—2 x 4 white plate
1—2 x 2 silver air scoop
1—1 x 2—2 x 2 lime green bracket, inverted
1—1 x 2 tile with cassette
1—1 x 1 tile with gauge
1—antenna
Assorted 1 x 1 round plates in colors of your choice

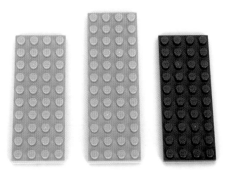

STEP 1: Begin the space cruiser with two 4 x 10 plates and a 4 x 12 plate.

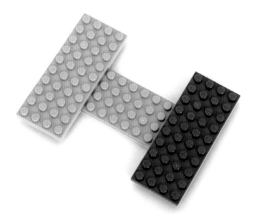

STEP 2: Attach the two 4 x 10 plates to the 4 x 12 plate as shown. There should be 6 studs exposed in between.

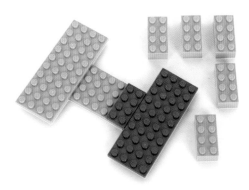

STEP 3: Add a dark gray 2 x 4 plate, and then find five 2 x 4 bricks.

STEP 4: Attach the 2 x 4 bricks as shown.

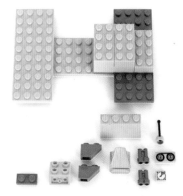

STEP 5: Gather the bricks shown.

STEP 6: Place the lime green bracket on the front of the speeder with the 1 x 2 dark gray plate just behind that. Then add the 2 x 4 slope.

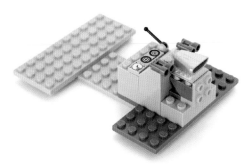

STEP 7: Add the 1 x 2 inverted slopes, the air scoop, the binoculars, the antenna and the tiles. If you don't have the exact tiles shown, get creative with what you have.

STEP 8: Add a purple 3 x 8 wedge plate and a black 2 x 4 wedge to the front on each side.

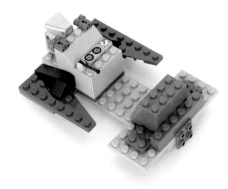

STEP 9: On the back of the space cruiser, attach a 1 x 4 plate, a 2 x 8 plate, two 1 x 2 plates and a 1 x 2—2 x 2 bracket.

STEP 10: Place two 1 x 6 plates on top of the bracket. Then add two 2 x 2 slopes (two bricks high) and two 1 x 2 bricks (two bricks high).

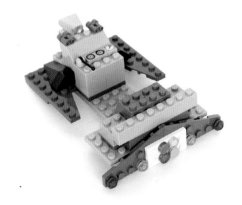

STEP 11: Add two 2 x 2 light gray bricks and a 1 x 8 brick.

STEP 12: Use two 3 x 6 wedge plates and a 2 x 4 white plate to create the back of the space cruiser. Add 1 x 1 round plates in any color.

STEP 13: Add two 10 x 3 wedge bricks to the sides of the space cruiser.

STEP 14: Gather the bricks shown for building the bottom of the space cruiser.

STEP 15: Attach two 2 x 2 plates to one set of the light gray inverted wedge bricks.

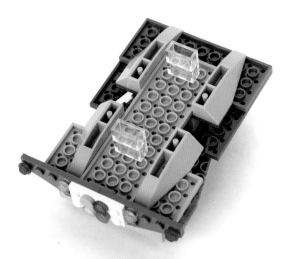

STEP 16: Place the inverted wedge bricks on the space cruiser as shown. Then add four 1 x 2 clear bricks. These will boost up the cruiser so that it appears to hover.

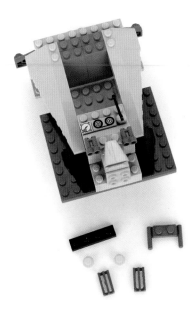

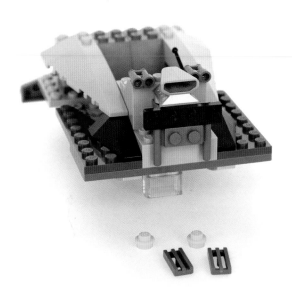

STEP 17: Gather a 1 x 4 black plate, two 1 x 1 yellow round plates, two 1 x 2 dark gray grills and a 1 x 2 dark gray plate with two handles.

STEP 18: Attach the 1 x 4 plate and the 1 x 2 plate with handles to the lime green bracket.

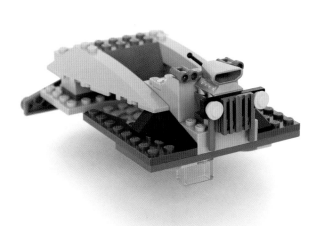

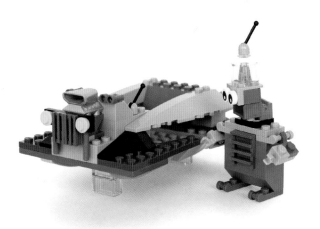

STEP 19: Add the headlights and the grills and the space cruiser is complete!

Pretend that Gadget is fixing up his space cruiser, ready to take off on an adventure! Or set up a crash scene with the space cruiser and the moon rover.

SLIME BLASTER

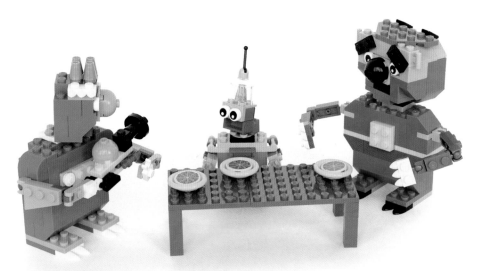

The moon rover was all repaired, the spaceship was functioning again, and the astronauts were preparing for their trek back to Earth. Grooby, Glump and Gadget were sitting around their table thinking. "I feel bad about blasting those poor astronauts with pizzas!" Grooby told the others.

"I actually feel the same way," grumbled Glump. "I think we've had enough of this crazy pizza blaster!"

"I'm glad you said that," said Grooby. "Let's just eat the pizzas. Look! I've already converted the pizza blaster to a slime blaster! Don't worry, though. It's not loaded."

"Oops, I guess it actually WAS loaded. Sorry about that, Glump!" Grooby exclaimed.

Gadget got up from the table. "You know what, guys? I have an idea," he said. "I'm going to go talk to those astronauts before they head back to Earth!"

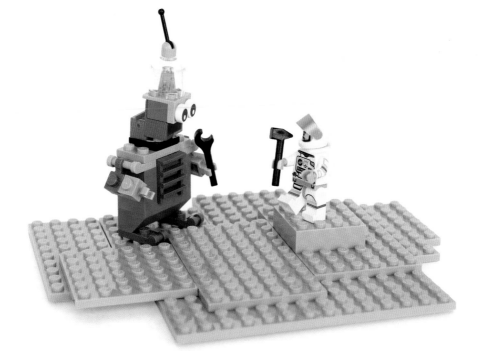

When the astronauts saw Gadget coming, they started to scramble into the spaceship!
Then they realized that he was not carrying any type of space blaster, and they slowly
crawled back out. The astronauts ended up exchanging some tips about tools with Gadget!

And that alien space cruiser turned out to be quite fun to fly!

DINOSAURS ON THE LOOSE

Build a LEGO world in which dinosaurs have come to life in the middle of town! In this adventure, kids travel back in time and find some interesting giant eggs. They transport the eggs back home and raise a whole pack of gigantic prehistoric pets, but those pets end up being a little more than they bargained for! Bring their story to life with a pteranodon who snatches things, a tyrannosaurus rex who chomps on a whole lot more than just food and more!

JOURNEY BACK IN TIME

It was a lazy summer afternoon with nothing interesting to do. Grant, Emily and Jason had already read every book in the house, and they were tired of throwing rocks in the creek. "Let's go exploring in the woods!" Grant suggested. Reluctantly, the others agreed. They had already found everything there was to discover in the woods, but they couldn't think of anything better to do.

Before they had ridden very far into the woods, the kids discovered a strange looking building overgrown with weeds. "Is this a house?" Grant wondered. "I don't remember ever seeing this before."

"It doesn't look like a house!" said Emily as she peered through the dirty glass. "It's a little room full of computers and stuff. It looks interesting!"

Grant lifted the rusty door. "Let's go in!" he told the others.

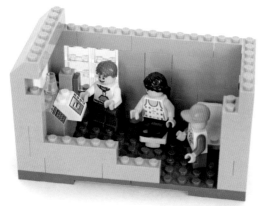

"You know," said Grant, "I know what this is! I think it's a time machine. There are all these dials here, and it looks like you can set the computer to travel to different periods of time."

"Let's try it!" said Emily.

"I don't know," said Jason. "I'm not sure if we should."

"It will be fine," Grant replied. "Look! This setting says, 'Time of the Din . . .' I can't see what's next. The screen is too dirty. Time of the Din . . . Could it be dinner? Time of the dinner?"

"Sounds good to me!" said Emily. "Let's go!"

Cautiously, Grant pushed the button.

The kids heard a strange whirring noise, followed by a series of loud bangs and bumps. Finally, everything was still. Grant, Emily and Jason carefully opened the door of the time machine and ventured out.

"Wow! Are these eggs?" said Emily.

"I don't know," said Grant. "They definitely look like eggs. But what creature would have eggs this large? I know! Let's take some of them home. We can let them hatch and find out what they are."

The other kids agreed, and they worked together to haul the enormous eggs into the time machine.

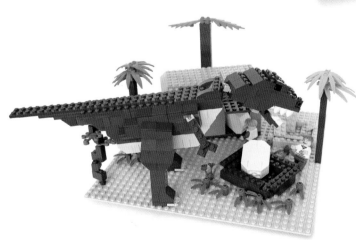

Suddenly, a large shadow seemed to overtake the children. Grant looked up and screamed as he found himself face-to-face with a gigantic tyrannosaurus rex!

"H-h-hey guys," he stammered. "I think we travelled to the time of the DINOSAURS!"

OLD FORGOTTEN TIME MACHINE

Build a time machine, and your LEGO minifigures can travel back to any period in history! Get creative with your bricks and windows to create a time machine that looks really epic. Add computer screens, buttons and levers. Your minifigures will be ready to head back to dinosaur time!

KEY ELEMENTS

TIME MACHINE
Various light gray bricks for the walls of the building
Various light gray plates for the roof
Various windows—get creative with what you have
2—8 x 8 dark gray plates
2—4 x 8 dark gray plates
1—4 x 6 dark gray plate
1—6 x 8 dark gray plate for the door
2—1 x 2 light gray Technic bricks
2—light gray Technic pins

2—1 x 2 dark gray plates with a pin hole
2—white chairs
2—2 x 2 white round plates
1—2 x 2 slope with computer screen
1—1 x 2 slope with computer screen
1—1 x 2 tile with buttons
1—1 x 1 translucent yellow cone
1—1 x 2 light gray slope, inverted

DINOSAUR NEST
1—6 x 8 brown plate for the bottom of the nest
Various brown bricks and plates for the nest

EGG STYLE 1
2—2 x 2 white slopes
2—2 x 4 white bricks
2—2 x 2 slopes, inverted

EGG STYLE 2
1—2 x 4 white double slope, inverted
1—2 x 2 white brick
2—1 x 2 white plates
2—2 x 4 bricks
2—2 x 2 slopes

STEP 1: The floor of the time machine is 8 x 16 studs wide. Use two 8 x 8 dark gray plates.

STEP 2: Connect the two 8 x 8 plates by attaching more dark gray plates underneath as shown.

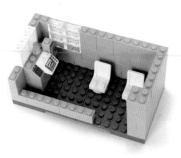

STEP 3: Build the walls of the time machine, leaving an opening 4 studs wide for the door. Place 2 x 2 round plates under the chairs to make them higher. There are two 2 x 4 gray bricks under the computers. Get creative with the windows and computer bricks you have. One wall is left open in this photo to allow a view of the computer area. Build up the final wall.

STEP 4: The bricks shown allow the door to swivel open and closed. You will need two sets of these bricks. Insert a gray connector pin into each 1 x 2 Technic brick, and the other ends into both 1 x 2 plates with a pin hole.

STEP 5: Attach the 1 x 2 Technic bricks to the door of the time machine.

STEP 6: Attach the two 1 x 2 plates with a pin hole to the time machine. The walls will need to be one brick lower than the rest of the wall height on either side of the door to allow for this.

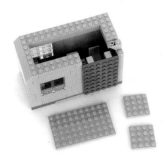

STEP 7: Use bricks that are two studs wide to build another layer onto the walls of the time machine. One end can be slope bricks. Leave the space above the door open. The bricks shown will be used for the roof.

STEP 8: Add the roof, and the time machine is complete!

The 1 x 2 inverted slope brick can be used to prop the door of the time machine open. Take off the inverted slope brick, open the door, and replace the brick. It will hold the door open. Now your minifigures are ready to travel back to the time of the dinosaurs!

Build a nest full of enormous dinosaur eggs for your minifigures to find after they travel back in time! The bottom of the nest is a 6 x 8 brown plate. Then add bricks and plates to build up the sides of the nest.

Gather the bricks shown to make a dinosaur egg. Simply attach them in a stack.

Here is another design for a dinosaur egg. Find a 2 x 4 double inverted slope (slopes on both sides), two 1 x 2 plates, a 2 x 2 brick, two 2 x 4 bricks and two 2 x 2 slopes.

Place the two 1 x 2 white plates on either side of the double inverted slope with the 2 x 2 brick in the middle.

Then add the two 2 x 4 bricks and the two 2 x 2 slope bricks. The nest is ready to be filled with eggs! What kinds of dinosaurs will hatch out of your eggs?

DINOSAURS ARE GREAT PETS!

For a while, the eggs just sat in the backyard, and the children began to wonder if there was anything in them at all. Then one day, they began to crack! Grant was there when they started hatching, and he quickly called the others to come and see!

"Wow, dinosaurs!" yelled Jason.

"Aren't they awesome?" exclaimed Grant.

"What will Mom think?" wondered Emily.

Having dinosaurs as pets made the three children the envy of the neighborhood. The baby dinosaurs followed the kids everywhere!

It was true, sometimes the dinos ended up knocking things over, but it was only because they were just babies—they were still learning!

(continued)

It was sort of like having toddlers around, except that these toddlers could each consume three packages of hot dogs at a time. They also liked pizza, steak, the flowers out of Mom's garden and the sheets off the clothesline. Mom was mad about the garden and the sheets, but the kids were positive that the dinosaurs would improve as they got older.

The dinosaurs grew and grew and grew to absolutely enormous sizes! Despite their hopes that adult dinosaurs would be easier to manage, the kids found that the full grown dinosaurs were still slightly messy and inconvenient. Well, to be honest, they were very messy and very inconvenient!

"Don't we have any mail?" asked Mom.

"Oh yes, we do!" said Emily. "It's just that Tabitha has it. She's up on the roof."

"AGAIN?" Mom shouted.

"Enough is enough!" Mom announced as she slammed a ladder against the side of the house.

"Where are you going with that rolling pin?" Emily asked.

"I'm chasing that pteranodon off the roof! For the last time!" Mom yelled.

It wasn't all bad, though, because Grant found that it was much easier to feed Spike the tyrannosaurus rex his meat from up on the ladder.

Unfortunately, however, Spike was hungry for a little more than a measly steak. He was tired of miniature-sized meals! The children gasped as they watched Spike take a massive bite out of the side of their house. The siding crumbled like a giant cracker under the dinosaur's massive jaws and roof tiles fell to the ground.

The children decided that this would be a good time to make themselves busy somewhere else before their mother decided to get rid of the dinosaurs for good. Mother checked the weather forecast and discovered that rain was on the way. She decided to waste no time in getting the roof put back on the house. The repair crew arrived right away!

BABY DINOSAURS

Create your own nursery with hatchling dinosaurs! Babies of any type of animal are always adorable, and these dinosaurs are no exception. Build miniature versions of a tyrannosaurus rex, brachiosaurus, raptor and pteranodon. Then find some LEGO food to feed them because these baby dinosaurs are always eating!

PARTS LIST

TYRANNOSAURUS REX

BROWN BRICKS

2—2 x 6 plates
4—2 x 4 plates
2—2 x 3 plates
4—2 x 2 plates
1—1 x 4 plate
4—1 x 3 plates
3—1 x 2 plates
1—2 x 4 brick
3—1 x 2 bricks
2—1 x 2 slopes
4—1 x 1 slopes, 30 degree
1—1 x 2 slope, 30 degree
1—2 x 2 inverted slope
2—1 x 2 inverted slopes
2—1 x 2 curved slopes

ASSORTED BRICKS

1—2 x 2 tan plate

1—2 x 4 tan plate
2—1 x 1 black round plates
4—1 x 1 white round plates

BRACHIOSAURUS

GREEN BRICKS

1—2 x 6 plate
9—2 x 4 plates
2—2 x 2 plates
15—1 x 2 bricks
2—1 x 2 curved slopes
2—1 x 2 slopes, 30 degree
1—2 x 2 inverted slope

ASSORTED BRICKS

1—2 x 6 tan brick
4—1 x 1 white round plates
2—1 x 1 black round plates

PTERANODON

DARK RED BRICKS

2—2 x 4 plates

2—3 x 3 corner wedge plates
1—2 x 4 wedge plate, right
1—2 x 4 wedge plate, left
1—1 x 4 plate
1—1 x 3 plate
1—1 x 2 plate
2—1 x 1 plates
2—1 x 2 plates with one stud on top

ASSORTED BRICKS

1—2 x 4 light gray plate
1—1 x 4 brown plate
1—2 x 2 brown plate
5—1 x 2 light gray plates with a socket on the end
3—1 x 2 dark gray plates with a ball on the side
2—1 x 2 dark gray plates with a ball on the end
2—1 x 1 purple slopes, 30 degree
1—1 x 1 translucent light blue round plate

TYRANNOSAURUS REX

STEP 1: Gather the bricks shown for building the tyrannosaurus rex's head.

STEP 2: Place two 1 x 1 white round plates, a 2 x 2 plate and a 1 x 2 slope on top of a 2 x 4 plate.

STEP 3: Add a 2 x 3 plate and a 1 x 2 brick. Place two more 1 x 1 white round plates under the 2 x 3 plate as teeth.

STEP 4: Build the rest of the head as shown.

STEP 5: Build the dinosaur's body. Place a 2 x 6 brown plate on top of a 2 x 2 tan plate and a 2 x 4 tan plate.

STEP 6: Add a 2 x 2 plate, a 2 x 4 plate, a 1 x 2 plate, a 1 x 4 plate and a 2 x 2 inverted slope.

STEP 7: Build up the body with a 2 x 4 plate and a 2 x 4 brick. Then add two 1 x 2 slopes and two 1 x 1 slopes.

STEP 8: Attach the head. Then add a 1 x 2 plate, a 2 x 4 plate and a 2 x 6 plate to the tail.

STEP 9: Add 1 x 3 plates for the arms, and add the legs. Each leg is a 1 x 3 plate, a 1 x 2 inverted slope and a 1 x 2 brick. Add a 2 x 2 plate and a 2 x 3 plate to the dinosaur's back. The tyrannosaurus rex is complete and ready to terrorize the neighborhood!

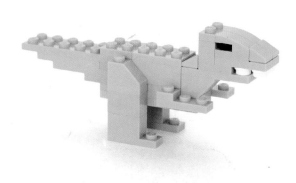

If you want to build a baby version of the raptor, use the pattern for the baby tyrannosaurus rex, but use lime green bricks instead of brown.

See if you can use the photo to build a brachiosaurus.

Then try building a baby pteranodon. This is one adorable dino! The design is very similar to the adult pteranodon.

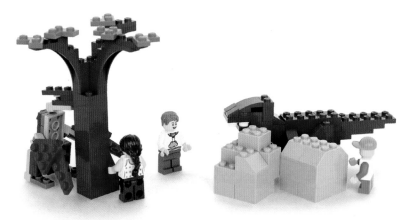

Now the kids and dinosaurs are ready to play! The dinos love a good game of hide-and-seek, although it's very difficult for them to hide!

SPIKE THE TYRANNOSAURUS REX

This massive tyrannosaurus rex looks as though he is ready to step through the pages of history and into real life! Well, LEGO life that is. He requires a lot of bricks, so build him any color you want, or make him multiple colors. His arms, legs and head are posable, and his mouth opens and closes so that he can eat LEGO houses or trees. Just don't let him eat your minifigures!

PARTS LIST

BROWN BRICKS
20—2 x 4 bricks
8—2 x 2 bricks
10—1 x 4 bricks
11—2 x 2 slopes
19—2 x 2 slopes, inverted
4—1 x 2 slopes, inverted
2—1 x 2 bricks
2—1 x 1 bricks with a stud on the side (headlight)
6—4 x 6 plates
2—4 x 4 plates
1—2 x 8 plate
3—2 x 6 plates

7—2 x 4 plates
12—1 x 4 plates
5—2 x 3 plates
5—2 x 2 plates
13—1 x 2 plates
4—2 x 2 corner plates
15—1 x 2 slopes, 30 degree
4—1 x 1 slopes, 30 degree
4—1 x 2 curved slopes
2—1 x 2 plates with a handle on the ends

TAN BRICKS
2—2 x 6 bricks
3—1 x 4 bricks
2—4 x 4 plates
2—2 x 6 plates

3—1 x 4 plates
10—2 x 2 slopes, inverted
2—1 x 2 plates with three claws

ASSORTED BRICKS
2—1 x 1 black round plates
5—1 x 2 dark gray plates with a ball on the side
7—1 x 1 white plates with a vertical tooth
4—1 x 1 white slopes, 30 degree
3—1 x 2 light gray plates with a socket on the side
2—1 x 2 light gray plates with a socket on the end
1—1 x 2 light gray plate with two clips

STEP 1: Start with the tyrannosaurus rex's head. Find a 4 x 6 plate and a 4 x 4 plate.

STEP 2: Place two 1 x 1 bricks with a stud on the side (headlight) on the end of the 4 x 4 plate, and place a 2 x 2 plate between them. Then add three 1 x 4 bricks, a 2 x 2 brick and a 2 x 4 brick.

STEP 3: Add a 2 x 2 slope between the two headlight bricks. Then add a 4 x 4 plate and two 2 x 2 slopes.

STEP 4: Add two 1 x 1 black round plates to be the eyes. Then add two 2 x 2 corner plates and a 1 x 4 plate. Find two 1 x 2 curved slopes and two 1 x 1 slopes (30 degree).

STEP 5: Place the slope bricks on the dinosaur's head as shown, and then find a 1 x 4 plate and two 2 x 2 plates.

STEP 6: Add one 2 x 2 plate and the 1 x 4 plate between and behind the eyes. Then add the second 2 x 2 plate.

STEP 7: Add two 2 x 2 slopes to the head.

STEP 8: Gather the bricks shown for the underside of the dinosaur's head.

STEP 9: Place a 1 x 2 plate with a socket on the side and three 1 x 2 plates on the end of the head farthest from the headlight bricks (the nostrils).

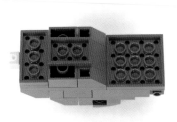

STEP 10: Add the rest of the bricks to the bottom of the head as shown.

STEP 11: Gather the bricks shown to complete the mouth of the tyrannosaurus rex.

STEP 12: Attach a 2 x 3 plate to the two 1 x 2 plates with handles on the end. Then add the 1 x 2 plate with clips. This will allow the mouth to open and close.

STEP 13: Add the 1 x 1 slopes to the lower jaw and the 1 x 1 plates with a vertical tooth to the head.

STEP 14: Attach the lower jaw, and the head is complete! Note that the head is very heavy and will flop forward in some positions. If you prefer the head to be stable, attach the head to the body instead of using the ball and socket joint.

STEP 15: Gather these bricks for the body of the tyrannosaurus rex and arrange them as shown.

STEP 16: Add two 4 x 4 plates, two 1 x 4 plates and two 1 x 2 plates with a ball on the side. These will hold the legs.

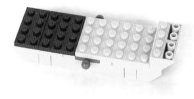

STEP 17: Add two 2 x 2 tan inverted slopes, two 2 x 6 tan plates, two 2 x 4 brown plates and a 1 x 4 brown plate.

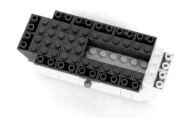

STEP 18: Add twelve 2 x 2 brown inverted slopes, a 2 x 4 brown brick and a 1 x 4 tan plate. The space shown in this step will be left hollow.

STEP 19: Add two more 2 x 2 tan inverted slopes and a layer of brown bricks as shown.

STEP 20: From left to right, add two 4 x 6 brown plates, a 1 x 4 tan brick and two 2 x 2 tan inverted slopes.

STEP 21: Place the dark gray 1 x 2 plates with a ball on the side just behind the tan bricks. Then add two 1 x 2 brown plates and two 1 x 4 brown plates. Note the position of the 1 x 4 brown plate toward the back of the body.

STEP 22: Add four 2 x 4 brown bricks in the space between the two 1 x 4 plates. Then add (from left to right) a 1 x 4 brick, a 2 x 4 brick, a 1 x 4 brick, a 2 x 4 plate, a 4 x 6 plate and two more 2 x 4 bricks.

STEP 23: Add a 2 x 4 brown plate and two 1 x 4 brown plates at the front of the body.

STEP 24: Place a dark gray 1 x 2 plate with a ball on the front to hold the head. Then add two 1 x 2 plates, a 2 x 6 plate and a 2 x 4 plate.

STEP 25: Add two 1 x 2 curved slopes, a 1 x 2 slope (30 degree) and a 1 x 4 plate to the neck of the dinosaur.

STEP 26: Use two 4 x 6 plates and a 2 x 3 plate to begin building the tail. Then find the brown plates shown.

STEP 27: Stack the plates as shown.

STEP 28: Attach the tail section to the body.

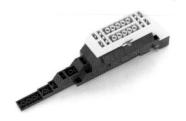

STEP 29: Turn the dinosaur body upside down and add a 2 x 4 brown brick, two 1 x 2 brown inverted slopes and two 2 x 2 brown inverted slopes.

STEP 30: Gather the bricks shown for completing the tyrannosaurus rex's body.

STEP 31: Add a 1 x 4 plate above each arm socket and a 1 x 4 brick just behind that on each side. Then fill in the body with slope bricks as shown.

STEP 32: Start building Spike's feet.

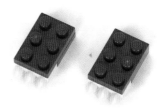

STEP 33: Add a 2 x 3 plate to each foot.

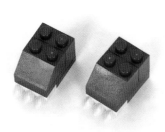

STEP 34: Add a 2 x 2 slope and a 1 x 2 brick to each foot.

STEP 35: Build up each leg with three 2 x 2 bricks.

STEP 36: Then add two 2 x 2 inverted slopes and a 2 x 4 brick to each leg.

STEP 37: Create the leg joint by adding a 1 x 2 plate with a socket on the side and three 1 x 2 plates to each leg.

STEP 38: Complete the legs by adding two 2 x 2 slopes, a 1 x 4 brick and two 1 x 2 slopes (30 degree) to each one. Then attach the legs to the body.

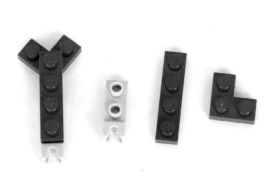

STEP 39: Build the arms as shown.

STEP 40: Attach the head and arms to the body and the tyrannosaurus rex is complete! Now your tyrannosaurus rex is ready to terrorize the town! Build some cars for him to step on, or pretend that he is chasing people and eating buildings!

TABITHA THE PTERANODON

This fun pteranodon is posable and pocket-sized! She can swoop and fly or sit on top of a building. Make her hunt for LEGO fish, or pretend that she is stealing mail out of the mailbox while your minifigures get more and more frustrated. You never can tell what a pteranodon will do!

PARTS LIST

DARK RED BRICKS
2—4 x 4 wedge plates
1—3 x 6 wedge plate, right
1—3 x 6 wedge plate, left
3—1 x 4 plates
1—2 x 2 plate with one stud on top
1—1 x 2 plate
1—1 x 3 plate

BROWN BRICKS
2—2 x 3 plates
1—1 x 6 plate
1—1 x 2 plate with one stud on top
1—1 x 1 slope, 30 degree

LIGHT GRAY BRICKS
1—2 x 6 plate
3—1 x 2 plates with a socket on the end
2—1 x 2 plates with a socket on the side

DARK GRAY BRICKS
4—1 x 2 plates with a ball on the end
1—1 x 2 plate with a ball on the side

ASSORTED BRICKS
2—1 x 1 purple slopes, 30 degree
1—1 x 1 translucent light blue round plate

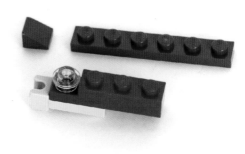

STEP 1: Gather a 1 x 6 brown plate, a 1 x 4 dark red plate, a 1 x 3 dark red plate, a 1 x 1 brown slope, a 1 x 2 light gray plate with a socket on the end and a 1 x 1 translucent blue round plate for the pteranodon's head.

STEP 2: Build Tabitha's head as shown. The light blue round plate is her eye.

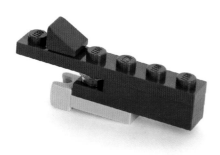

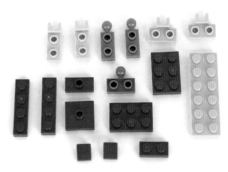

STEP 3: Add the 1 x 6 brown plate and the 1 x 1 brown slope to the head.

STEP 4: Gather the bricks shown for the pteranodon's body.

STEP 5: Attach the 2 x 3 brown plate to the underside of the 2 x 6 light gray plate.

STEP 6: Flip the bricks over to the other side and add two 1 x 4 dark red plates, two 1 x 2 light gray plates with a socket on the side, a 1 x 2 dark red plate and a 1 x 2 dark gray plate with a ball on the side.

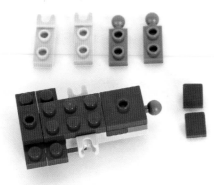

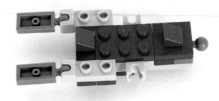

STEP 7: Add a 1 x 2 brown plate with one stud on top, a 2 x 3 brown plate and a 2 x 2 dark red plate with one stud on top.

STEP 8: Attach the two 1 x 1 purple slopes, the two 1 x 2 light gray plates with a socket on the end and the two 1 x 2 dark gray plates with a ball on the end. The dark gray plates are Tabitha's feet.

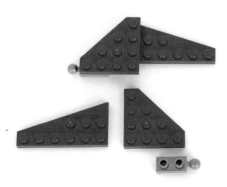

STEP 9: Build the wings as shown. Each wing has a 1 x 2 dark gray plate with a ball on the end, a 3 x 6 wedge plate and a 4 x 4 wedge plate.

STEP 10: Attach the wings and the head to the body, and Tabitha the pteranodon is complete!

Now Tabitha is ready to swoop through the neighborhood stealing mail from the mailboxes! Or pretend that she is hunting for fish in a river or perching on top of a house.

TWO STORY HOUSE

Use your LEGO bricks to create a cozy home for your minifigures! Make it a two story house by adding a layer of light gray plates between the floors. Build furniture such as a table for the kitchen, a bed and a desk, and your LEGO minifigures will be living in style. As sturdy as this home looks, however, it can still become a snack for a hungry T rex!

KEY ELEMENTS

HOUSE
1—tan baseplate
Various tan bricks
Various light gray plates for the second story floor and the sidewalk
8—1 x 4 windows, 3 bricks high
Dark blue slopes for roof tiles
1—1 x 4 door, 6 bricks high
Brown plates for the flower bed
Trees and bushes

MAILBOX
2—1 x 1 dark gray round bricks
1—2 x 2 x 2 red box container with door
1—2 x 2 red brick with curved top

TABLE
1—4 x 6 brown plate
4—1 x 1 brown round bricks
4—1 x 1 brown round plates
2—brown chairs
2—2 x 2 brown round plates

SHELF
3—2 x 4 light gray plates
6—1 x 2 light gray bricks

BED
3—2 x 4 light blue bricks
2—2 x 4 light blue plates
1—2 x 4 white plate
1—2 x 4 white tile

LAMP
1—1 x 4 light gray antenna
1—1 x 1 translucent yellow round plate
1—2 x 2 white dish

DESK
1—2 x 6 brown plate
4—1 x 1 brown round bricks
1—brown chair

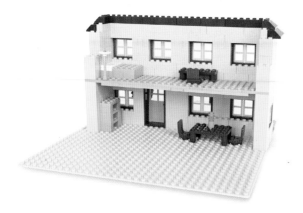

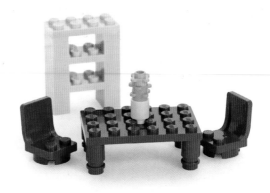

The back of the house has been left open to make the rooms more accessible and easier to play with. Use light gray plates to create a second story. Choose the largest ones you have, and then add more plates underneath those to hold them together.

Build a simple dining table and chairs. Each table leg has one 1 x 1 brown round brick and one 1 x 1 brown round plate.

Furnish the bedroom with a twin bed, a lamp and a desk with a chair. To build the lamp, attach a 2 x 2 white dish to the top of a gray antenna. The 1 x 1 yellow translucent round plate is just sitting on top of the antenna.

Pretend that the tyrannosaurus rex has taken some gigantic bites out of the house! Remove bricks, but also add a 1 x 1 brick with a stud on the side.

Then attach a 2 x 4 slope to the 1 x 1 brick so that it appears to be hanging off the house. Now pretend that a construction crew is coming to repair the house. Or send the tyrannosaurus rex on another rampage and let him tear the house down!

DOWNTOWN DISASTER

"You know," said Grant after the house was repaired, "Let's go find something to do and leave Mom alone. We'll go downtown to the candy store."

Emily and Jason agreed, and they set off on their way.

"Aw, I think Speedy looks lonely," said Jason. "And bored!"

Grant had a terrific idea. He could give the raptor some skateboards to use as roller skates! That would be so much more fun than walking to town.

Speedy, who was quite a bit nimbler on his feet than the massive Spike, took to the skates like a duck to water! Before long, the kids and the dino were all zooming toward town.

"You can stop now!" Grant yelled to his prehistoric pet. "The candy store is right here!" But Speedy wasn't stopping! All three kids started yelling, "STOP!" at the top of their lungs!

But it was too late . . .

Grant, Emily and Jason watched in horror as their raptor collided with Dr. Russell's very nice convertible sports car. Dr. Russell looked extremely angry.

"Boy, are we in trouble," groaned Grant.

Mother had been having lunch at the Pizza Café with a friend, and she came running when she heard the crash. Officer Jones arrived quickly to sort out the accident. "Is this your dinosaur, ma'am?" he asked Mother.

"Yes, unfortunately it is," she said with a sigh. "We will be happy to pay for the damage, and we will make sure that this never happens again."

(continued)

"Yes, you had better see to it that it doesn't happen again!" said Officer Jones as he hastily filled out an accident report. Suddenly, he stopped. "Is that your dinosaur also? The one eating leaves off our town's oldest and most historic tree?"

Mother's face turned red as she slowly nodded yes.

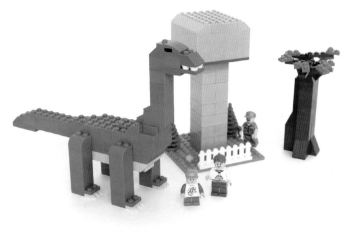

Grant and Jason quickly began walking Wesley the brachiosaurus home while Emily stayed back to help Mother. Everything was going smoothly until they stopped by the old water tower to watch planes taking off at the airport.

"Look over there!" yelled Grant. "That 747 is awesome!"

Unfortunately, Wesley turned to look too. And as he turned his body, his massive tail slammed into the side of the water tower. It doesn't take much imagination to figure out what happened next . . .

MAIN STREET

Create a cheerful downtown scene with a doctor's office, a candy store and a pizza café. Minifigures will enjoy riding their bikes to buy a treat at the candy store! Build a water tower for your town with a hilarious twist. The pieces are merely stacked so that the brachiosaurus can knock it down with one swipe of his giant tail!

KEY ELEMENTS

Bricks and slopes in various colors for creating buildings

Small baseplates or large plates for the buildings

Various windows and doors

Chairs

4 x 4 round bricks for the pizza shop tables

Food accessories—pizzas, popsicles, etc. (get creative with what you have!)

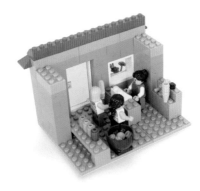

Build a cheerful candy store with flowers out front and colorful shelves inside. Make a ledge for the flowers with a 4 x 4 plate. Two rows of studs stick out past the wall of the building. A clear door makes it easy to peek inside and see all the fun details.

Build a soft-serve ice cream machine with gray bricks and a gray nozzle. Use 1 x 1 tan cones for ice cream cones, and fill them with 1 x 1 round plates in white, brown or pink.

The pizza shop is a cozy place to eat with friends. Build an outdoor table out of a 4 x 4 round brick and an umbrella.

A 4 x 4 round plate on top of a 2 x 2 brick makes a great table for indoors. If you have enough bricks, make several tables so that the shop can handle plenty of customers.

The town water tower looks normal, but it has a funny twist!

Build the water tower in sections, with tiles on top of each section. This allows the pieces to sit on top of each other, but they won't connect.

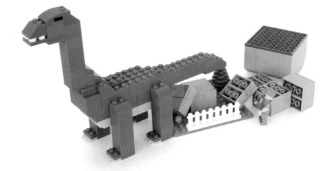

Watch out for the dinosaur as he swings his large tail around!

Yikes, there goes the water tower! Try making a different type of tower or even a building that falls down in the same way. Dinosaur destruction is a lot of fun!

WESLEY THE BRACHIOSAURUS

The brachiosaurus, being a plant eater, makes a much better pet than a tyrannosaurus rex. Or does he? He's got a big appetite, which means that the trees in the yard are going to be bare in no time! And watch out for that enormous tail—he can knock down buildings with that!

PARTS LIST

GREEN BRICKS
1—4 x 10 plate
2—2 x 8 plates
1—2 x 6 plate
1—4 x 4 plate
9—2 x 4 plates
11—2 x 2 plates
1—1 x 4 plate
5—1 x 2 plates
1—1 x 2 plate with one stud on top

8—2 x 4 bricks
1—2 x 3 brick
25—2 x 2 bricks
1—1 x 4 brick
4—2 x 3 bricks with a curved end
3—1 x 2 bricks
4—2 x 2 slopes
4—1 x 2 slopes
4—2 x 2 slopes, inverted
2—1 x 2 slopes, 30 degree
2—1 x 2 x 1 panels
2—1 x 2 curved slopes

TAN BRICKS
1—2 x 6 brick
4—1 x 4 bricks
2—2 x 4 plates
1—2 x 2 brick
2—2 x 2 slopes, inverted
4—1 x 2 plates with 3 claws

ASSORTED BRICKS
2—black 1 x 1 round plates
4—white 1 x 1 white round plates

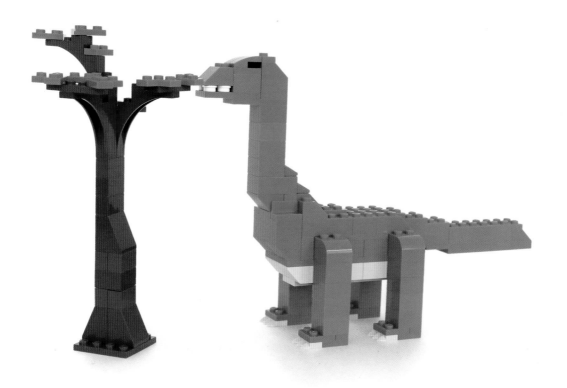

STEP 1: Start with two 2 x 4 tan plates.

STEP 2: Add two 2 x 2 inverted slopes, a 2 x 6 brick and a 2 x 2 brick.

STEP 3: Place a 4 x 10 green plate on top of the tan bricks. Then find four 1 x 4 tan bricks.

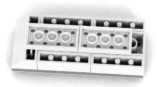

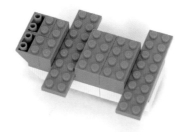

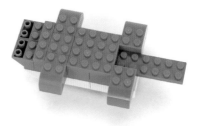

STEP 4: Turn the body of the brachiosaurus upside down and add the four 1 x 4 bricks as shown.

STEP 5: Turn the body over and add two 2 x 2 green inverted slopes on the front of the body (the end with the tan inverted slopes). Then add two 1 x 2 bricks, a 2 x 8 plate, two 2 x 4 bricks and another 2 x 8 plate.

STEP 6: From left to right, add a 1 x 4 green plate, two 2 x 3 green bricks with curved ends, a 2 x 2 green brick, a 4 x 4 green plate, two more 2 x 3 green bricks with curved ends and a 2 x 6 green plate.

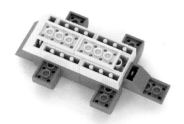

STEP 7: Turn the dinosaur's body over and add a 2 x 2 green inverted slope under the tail.

STEP 8: Turn the body back over and add (from left to right) four 2 x 4 bricks, a 1 x 4 brick, a 2 x 2 brick and a 2 x 4 brick.

STEP 9: Add a 2 x 4 green plate to the front end (left). Then add two 1 x 2 slopes, a 2 x 4 plate and a 2 x 2 plate to the tail end.

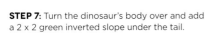

STEP 10: Start on the brachiosaurus' neck by adding a 2 x 4 plate, a 2 x 2 inverted slope, a 1 x 2 brick and a 2 x 3 brick.

STEP 11: Add a 2 x 2 slope and a 1 x 2 slope to the base of the neck. Then add four 2 x 2 bricks.

STEP 12: Gather the bricks shown.

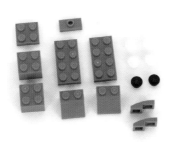

STEP 13: Add the two panels to either side of the neck. Then add the 2 x 2 plate behind the neck. Attach the two 1 x 2 slopes and the 1 x 2 slope (30 degree).

STEP 14: Gather the bricks shown for the brachiosaurus' head.

STEP 15: Attach one 2 x 4 plate to the other so that they overlap by 4 total studs. Then add four 1 x 1 white round plates to be teeth.

STEP 16: Add the two 2 x 2 bricks.

STEP 17: Complete the head as shown. The 2 x 2 plate is under the eyes.

STEP 18: Gather the bricks shown for the tail.

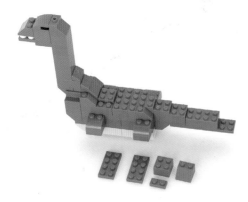

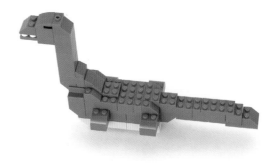

STEP 19: Attach two 2 x 4 plates and a 2 x 4 brick.

STEP 20: Build the end of the tail. If you don't have the bricks shown, get creative with what you have.

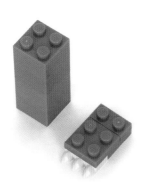

STEP 21: Build the legs. Each leg has a 1 x 2 tan plate with three claws and a 2 x 2 plate on the bottom. Then add a 2 x 2 plate and a 1 x 2 plate. Complete the leg with four 2 x 2 bricks.

STEP 22: Attach the legs, and your brachiosaurus is ready to go stomping through town! Build him a tree to nibble, or pretend that he is knocking down buildings with his long tail.

Make it look like the brachiosaurus is really eating tree branches by removing one of his front teeth. Then you can attach a tree branch in his mouth.

SPEEDY THE RAPTOR

Speedy is a nimble dinosaur and a fast hunter. You might want to make sure that he's not around while the family is grilling steak! Pose his arms and legs so that he can roller skate on skateboards or spread his limbs out as he crashes into a car!

PARTS LIST

LIME GREEN BRICKS

5—2 x 4 bricks
8—2 x 2 bricks
4—1 x 2 bricks
2—2 x 2 slopes
3—2 x 2 slopes, inverted
6—2 x 4 plates
5—2 x 6 plates
4—2 x 3 plates
3—2 x 2 plates
2—1 x 6 plates
4—1 x 4 plates

2—1 x 3 plates
3—1 x 2 plates
2—1 x 1 plates
4—1 x 2 plates with one stud on top
2—1 x 1 slopes, 30 degree
10—1 x 2 slopes, 30 degree
6—1 x 2 curved slopes

LIGHT GRAY BRICKS

1—2 x 8 plate
2—4 x 4 plates
3—2 x 4 plates
1—2 x 2 plate
1—2 x 2 slope, inverted

1—2 x 3 slope, inverted
2—1 x 2 slopes, inverted
4—1 x 2 plates with a socket on the side

DARK GRAY BRICKS

2—2 x 2 plates
2—1 x 2 plates with three claws
2—1 x 2 plates with a ball on the end
2—1 x 2 plates with a ball on the side
2—2 x 2 corner plates

ASSORTED BRICKS

4—1 x 1 brown slopes, 30 degree
4—1 x 1 white plates
2—1 x 1 translucent red plates

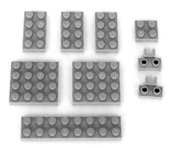

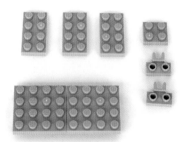

STEP 1: Gather the bricks shown for the raptor's body.

STEP 2: Attach both 4 x 4 plates to the top of the 2 x 8 plate.

STEP 3: Add three 2 x 4 plates and two 1 x 2 plates with a socket on the side as shown.

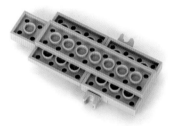

STEP 4: Turn the body over and add the 2 x 2 plate at the front (far left).

STEP 5: Turn the body back over. Add a 1 x 4 lime green plate on each side.

STEP 6: Add four 2 x 4 lime green bricks, a 1 x 2 lime green brick and a 2 x 3 light gray inverted slope.

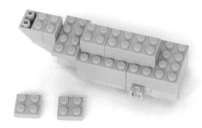

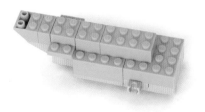

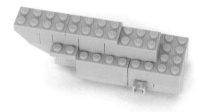

STEP 7: Continue building the body with a 2 x 4 brick, a 2 x 2 brick, a 2 x 4 plate, a 1 x 2 brick and a 2 x 2 inverted slope. Then find two 2 x 2 plates.

STEP 8: Stack the two 2 x 2 plates and place them on top of the 2 x 4 plate from the previous step.

STEP 9: Attach two 2 x 4 plates to the top of the body.

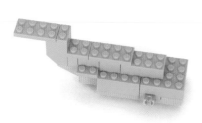

STEP 10: Build the neck by adding a 2 x 2 brick. Then add a 1 x 2 plate and a 2 x 4 plate.

STEP 11: Add a 2 x 3 plate and four 1 x 1 white round plates to the head. Then add a 1 x 2 plate and a 2 x 4 plate. Gather the bricks shown.

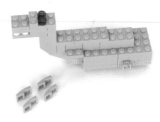

STEP 12: Place a 2 x 3 plate and a 2 x 2 plate on top of the head. Then add a 1 x 2 plate and two 1 x 1 translucent red round plates for eyes.

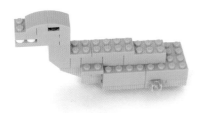

STEP 13: Finish up the head with four 1 x 2 curved slopes.

STEP 14: Start building the tail. Add two 2 x 6 plates and a 2 x 4 plate. Place a 1 x 6 plate on each side of the body.

STEP 15: Add three more 2 x 6 plates to the tail. Add five 1 x 2 slopes along both sides of the back.

STEP 16: Turn the raptor over and add a 2 x 2 light gray inverted slope to the underside of the tail.

STEP 17: Build the raptor's feet. Each foot has a 2 x 2 dark gray plate, a 1 x 2 dark gray plate with three claws and a 2 x 3 lime green plate.

STEP 18: Add three 2 x 2 bricks to each leg.

STEP 19: Place a 2 x 2 inverted slope and a 1 x 2 brick on the top of each leg.

STEP 20: Add to each leg: a 1 x 1 plate, a 1 x 3 plate and a 1 x 2 plate with a ball on the side.

STEP 21: Complete the legs by adding a 2 x 2 slope and a 1 x 1 slope to each one.

STEP 22: Assemble the arms as shown. Each arm has a 1 x 2 light gray inverted slope, a 1 x 2 light gray plate with a socket on the side, a 1 x 2 dark gray plate with a ball on the end, a 1 x 4 lime green plate, a 1 x 2 lime green curved slope and a 2 x 2 dark gray corner plate.

STEP 23: Build spikes for the raptor's back. Use a 1 x 2 plate with one stud on top and a 1 x 1 slope for each spike.

STEP 24: Attach the spikes and the raptor is complete! Now find some LEGO skate boards for him to ride, or pretend that he is stomping on cars as he runs through town. Raptors are fast and tricky creatures!

SPORTY CONVERTIBLE

Build a sporty convertible car for your minifigures to cruise around town. It's a great looking car that will make all the other minifigures jealous! Well, until a dinosaur lands on it and destroys it, that is . . .

PARTS LIST

BLUE BRICKS
1—2 x 4 plate
4—1 x 4 plates
6—1 x 2 plates
2—1 x 1 bricks
2—1 x 4 bricks
2—1 x 2—1 x 4 brackets
4—1 x 2 curved slopes

1—car door, left
1—car door, right

ASSORTED BRICKS
1—4 x 12 dark gray vehicle base
4—4 x 2½ x 1⅔ dark gray vehicle mudguards with arch
1—2 x 4 light gray plate
1—1 x 4 light gray plate
1—1 x 2 light gray grill

1—1 x 2 white tile
2—1 x 1 translucent yellow round plates
2—1 x 1 translucent red round plates
2—2 x 2 black plates with two axles
4—wheels
1—windshield, 3 x 4 x 1⅓
1—white chair
1—steering wheel

STEP 1: Start with a 4 x 12 vehicle base.

STEP 2: Add four vehicle mudguards, two 1 x 2 blue plates and two 1 x 2—1 x 4 brackets.

STEP 3: Place a 1 x 4 plate on top of the bracket in the front. Then add two 1 x 4 blue plates behind the mudguards. Add a 1 x 4 brick in front of the mudguards on the back end of the car.

STEP 4: Add four 1 x 2 curved slopes to the front of the car, and add the doors.

STEP 5: Add a 1 x 4 blue plate just behind the curved slopes. Then add three 1 x 2 blue plates.

STEP 6: Place a 1 x 1 brick behind each door. Then add a 2 x 4 blue plate and a 1 x 4 blue brick.

STEP 7: Attach the steering wheel to the 1 x 2 blue plate. Then add the steering wheel, chair, windshield and light gray plates to the car.

STEP 8: Add yellow headlights and a grill to the front of the car.

STEP 9: Place a 1 x 2 white tile on the back to be a license plate. Then add red taillights and assemble the wheels.

STEP 10: Attach the wheels, and the car is complete! Now it's ready to cruise around town. Just be careful where you park the car! Make sure that there are no enormous reptiles nearby!

DINO TRAINING

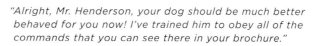

"Alright, Mr. Henderson, your dog should be much better behaved for you now! I've trained him to obey all of the commands that you can see there in your brochure."

"Thanks so much, Ms. Swift," Mr. Henderson replied. "What a relief to know that my dog won't be dragging me down the sidewalk on his leash anymore!"

"Excuse me," started Mother, a little hesitantly. "I hear you're an excellent pet obedience coach, and I was wondering . . . Have you ever worked with, uh, dinosaurs? You see, my kids have several dinosaurs as pets, and well, I CAN'T TAKE IT ANYMORE! I thought that you might be able to help. Do you think you can do it?"

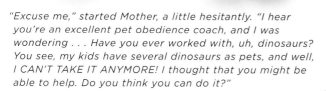

"Well, to be honest I've never worked with dinosaurs before. But I think I'm up for the challenge!" Ms. Swift responded.

"We'll get started now! Let's get moving, dinosaurs! And T Rex, KEEP YOUR TEETH TO YOURSELF!"

"Thank you!" Mother shouted above the noise.

"The first thing you must learn, dinos, is to be useful! Not destructive! Brachiosaurus, it's time for school bus training. Take those kids to school! Stand up tall! Look straight ahead! Good job!"

Everyone could tell that owning dinosaurs as pets was going to work out quite nicely after all!

TEX ALEXANDER

AND THE QUEST FOR THE CRYSTAL BUNNY

Tex Alexander is a top-rate detective and adventurer who can get to the bottom of any case! Tex and his sidekick Bill have traveled the globe solving mysteries, recovering treasure and tracking down bad guys. Build along with Tex and Bill as they travel to the Palace Ruins of Cape Cuckoo in search of the missing piece of the Crystal Bunny. Will they find the missing piece before the villain Vincent Drake gets his evil hands on it? Will they collect the $200,000 reward? Build and find out!

THE MISSING PIECE

Tex Alexander was sitting at his desk one gray October day when the door to his detective office suddenly swung open. In walked two men whom Tex had never seen before.

"We've come from the National Museum of Science and History," the older gentleman said. "I'm Dr. Cooper, and this is another member of our staff. His name is Aaron Watts. We're here on assignment from the museum. We hear that you're a detective of the adventurous sort."

"Yes, you could say that," said Tex. "Please sit down."

"Here's the issue," Dr. Cooper began. "The museum has acquired an extremely valuable Crystal Bunny from the ancient Palace Ruins of Cape Cuckoo. However, a piece of the statue is missing. Without the piece, the bunny would be an embarrassment to display! If we were able to acquire the missing piece, the bunny could easily become the most popular exhibit in museum history, bringing in thousands of dollars in revenue. We need you to travel to Cape Cuckoo and search through the Palace Ruins for the missing piece. But there are two more problems. One is that we're not sure exactly what the missing piece looks like. The other problem is that someone else wants the piece. Vincent Drake."

"You see," Dr. Cooper continued, "he's on a quest to find it, and rumor has it that he and his henchmen plan to steal the Crystal Bunny once he has the final piece. I'm afraid he's quite a dangerous guy. Are you up for the mission?"

Tex leaned back in his chair.

"I don't know," he sighed. "It sounds like a lot of hassle. I'll have to secure some type of aircraft, fly to Cape Cuckoo and search for the ruins. There will probably be snakes and other creatures and poisonous jungle plants. Then I'll have to find the missing piece without even knowing what it looks like, while avoiding a bad guy with a gun who wants the missing piece more than I do."

"We can pay $200,000," Dr. Cooper said.

"Deal," said Tex.

Tex called for Bill, his sidekick. "Come on, Bill! We've got a job to do!"

"Where are we headed?" asked Bill.

"To Cape Cuckoo," answered Tex. "But first, we're stopping by the museum to look at this Crystal Bunny."

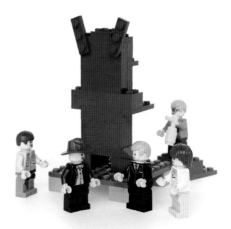

"Well, as you can see, this is the magnificent Crystal Bunny!" Dr. Cooper announced.

"Um," said Tex, "It doesn't look like a Crystal Bunny! I'd say it's more like a chocolate bunny!"

"Quite the contrary," Dr. Cooper gasped. "This is rare earth-colored crystal found only on Cape Cuckoo!"

"Ah, I see," said Tex. "Bill, let's get to it!"

DETECTIVE OFFICE

Create a detective office that looks like it came to life from the pages of a legendary tale! Construct the building using bricks with brick line details for added personality, and then add a detective sign above the door. Your adventure hero will be able to crack his toughest cases in this well-equipped office!

KEY ELEMENTS

OFFICE BUILDING
1—baseplate
1—1 x 4 door, 6 bricks high
4—1 x 4 windows, 3 bricks high
Various tan bricks
1 x 2 gray bricks, modified with brick lines
25—4 x 4 tan plates for the floor
2—brown chairs
2—2 x 2 brown round plates

OFFICE SIGN
1—1 x 4 brown plate
1—1 x 2 brown plate
1—1 x 2—2 x 2 tan bracket

1—2 x 4 tan plate
1—1 x 1 black plate with a clip on top
1—magnifying glass

DESK CHAIR
2—4 x 4 brown plates
1—1 x 6 brown plate
2—1 x 3 brown plates
1—2 x 2 brown plate
3—1 x 2 brown plates
2—1 x 4 bricks
1—2 x 2 turntable plate
1—1 x 4 double curved slope

DESK
2—4 x 6 brown plates
2—2 x 6 brown plates

5—1 x 4 brown bricks
5—1 x 2 brown bricks
Various bricks for desk accessories

PHONE
1—2 x 2 black plate
1—1 x 2 black plate with one stud on top
2—1 x 1 slopes, 30 degree
1—1 x 1 tile with a clip on top
1—1 x 3 phone handset

SHELF
3—2 x 8 brown plates
12—1 x 2 brown bricks
2—1 x 2 brown plates
Accessories—cups, jewels, maps, etc.

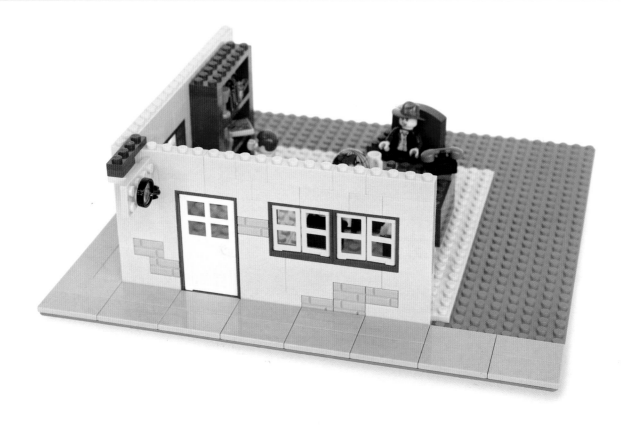

Tex Alexander's office is furnished with a large desk and extra chairs for visitors.

Gather the bricks shown to build the sign.

Attach the 2 x 4 plate to the tan bracket, and place a 1 x 2 brown plate on the top of the bracket.

Add a 1 x 4 brown plate on the top. This will attach the sign to the building. Then add a 1 x 1 black tile with a clip and the magnifying glass. If you don't have a magnifying glass, try using a tile with a map instead.

Build a bookcase using 2 x 8 plates and 1 x 2 bricks. The top shelf has two added 1 x 2 plates to allow room for the tall bottles. Look through your LEGO accessories for items that would look good in an adventurer's office. Display jewels, bottles, maps or books.

Gather these bricks to build an armchair that swivels

Stack the two 4 x 4 plates. Then add a 1 x 6 plate.

Place two 1 x 4 bricks, a 1 x 2 plate and a 1 x 4 double curved slope on top of the 1 x 6 plate.

Attach a 1 x 3 plate and a 1 x 2 plate to make each arm.

Place the turntable on top of the 2 x 2 plate, and then attach these to the bottom of the chair to make it swivel.

Gather the bricks shown to build the desk.

Connect the two 4 x 6 plates by attaching the 2 x 6 plates to the underside.

Attach bricks to the underside of the desk as shown. The remaining bricks go on either side of the underside of the desk.

The completed desk and chair should look like this.

Gather the bricks shown for building the phone.

Assemble the phone as shown.

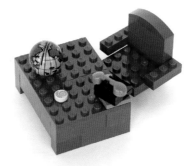

Look through your LEGO bricks for accessories for the desk such as a coffee mug, globe and map.

Now your adventurer is ready for his next quest! Find some minifigures who need his help, or pretend that he is answering an important phone call about a case that needs to be solved!

FLIGHT TO CAPE CUCKOO

"Bill," said Tex, "You should be amazed and impressed! I have managed to secure us the most advanced biplane for our flight to Cape Cuckoo. The Cape is not exactly equipped with a landing strip, but we should be quite all right with the state-of-the-art landing gear on this plane!"

At that moment, a very stern looking man came zooming up in his roadster.

"You must be Drake," said Tex.

"That I am," Drake answered. "If I were you, I'd walk away from that plane right now. You and your buddy are just wasting your time."

"Your intimidation does nothing to thwart our mission," Tex announced. "I am quite confident that my partner and I have the skills necessary to come out on top."

"Well," Drake sneered, "we shall see about that, won't we! Just wait until you see who has that missing piece in their hands! And it won't be you!"

With that, Drake roared off in his roadster. Tex and Bill silently boarded the plane.

"Do you have the map, Bill?" Tex asked.

"I've got it! Let's go find the missing piece of the chocolate bunny! I mean, Crystal Bunny!"

With a loud roar of the engine, the plane took off at lightning speed.

CLASSIC BIPLANE

Build a 1930s style biplane! The structure of the biplane with one wing over the other made this type of aircraft both strong and lightweight. However, the extra bracing needed between the two wings caused excess drag, and the biplane design was replaced almost exclusively by the monoplane during the 1930s. Still, the biplane has a fun and classic look which people still enjoy today! This LEGO biplane is ready to transport your heroes to Cape Cuckoo just as quick as a flash.

PARTS LIST

LIGHT GRAY BRICKS
2—6 x 10 plates
4—4 x 4 plates
2—2 x 4 plates
2—4 x 10 plates
2—1 x 2 bricks, two bricks high
2—1 x 2 bricks
1—2 x 2 brick
2—2 x 2 slopes
1—1 x 2—2 x 2 bracket, inverted

RED BRICKS
1—4 x 6 plate
5—4 x 4 plates
1—2 x 10 plate
3—2 x 8 plates
3—2 x 6 plates
2—1 x 8 plates

1—2 x 4 plate
4—1 x 4 plates
3—2 x 2 plates
7—1 x 2 plates
2—2 x 4 bricks
3—2 x 2 bricks
1—2 x 2 plate with a vertical pin
1—1 x 4 brick
2—1 x 1 bricks
2—2 x 2 slopes, inverted
4—1 x 2 slopes, inverted
1—2 x 4 slope, 45 degree double inverted
2—1 x 2 plates with one stud on top
2—1 x 3 slopes
2—1 x 4 x 1 panels
4—1 x 1 corner panels
2—2 x 2 tiles
3—1 x 2 slopes, 30 degree

ASSORTED BRICKS
1—3 x 8 white wedge plate, right
1—3 x 8 white wedge plate, left
1—4 x 1 x 3 white tail
1—3 x 12 dark red wedge plate, right
1—3 x 12 dark red wedge plate, left
1—2 x 4 dark gray plate
1—2 x 4 dark gray air scoop
2—1 x 2 dark gray plates with one stud on top
1—1 x 2 tile with gauges
2—1 x 4 black plates with angled tubes
3—2 x 2 light gray plates with plane wheel single holder
3—wheel centers, small with stub axles
3—tires, 14 mm x 4 mm
1—propeller
1—2 x 2 cone, truncated

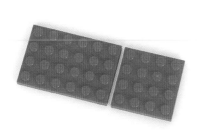

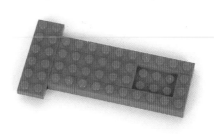

STEP 1: Start with a 4 x 4 plate and a 4 x 6 plate.

STEP 2: Add a 2 x 6 plate, three 1 x 2 plates and two 1 x 8 plates as shown. Then find another 2 x 6 plate and a 2 x 4 dark gray plate.

STEP 3: Stack the dark gray 2 x 4 plate and the red 2 x 6 plate and place them next to the other section. They are not attached yet.

STEP 4: Place two 4 x 4 plates over the red section, starting on the end with the open area. Each wing is a 4 x 4 light gray plate, a 4 x 10 light gray plate and a 3 x 12 dark red wedge plate. Attach the wings to the other end. This will attach the two sections of the body to each other.

STEP 5: Gather the bricks shown to build the engine and propeller.

STEP 6: Attach the red 4 x 4 plate to the light gray 2 x 4 plate so that four studs are exposed.

STEP 7: Build the engine as shown.

STEP 8: Stack the two 1 x 2 plates on top of the 1 x 4 plate. Turn the engine over and add the light gray bracket and the red plates to the underside of the engine as shown.

STEP 9: Attach the 2 x 2 plate with a pin and the propeller to the light gray bracket.

STEP 10: Attach the engine to the body of the plane.

STEP 11: Add two 1 x 4 red plates, one on each side of the cockpit. Then add a 4 x 4 plate and two 1 x 3 slopes.

STEP 12: Place a 2 x 2 red plate and a 2 x 8 red plate on top of a 2 x 10 red plate. Or simply stack two 2 x 10 plates. Attach these to two 3 x 8 wedge plates to build the tail.

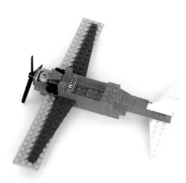

STEP 13: Add a 2 x 6 red plate, two 1 x 2 red plates with one stud on top and two 1 x 2 dark gray plates with one stud on top.

STEP 14: Add two 1 x 4 x 1 red panels, two 1 x 1 red corner panels and a 1 x 4 red brick to the plane. Place a 1 x 1 red brick on each side of the plane next to the dashboard. Add a white tail, two 2 x 2 tiles and a 1 x 2 red slope to the tail. Then find a red 2 x 4 plate and a red 1 x 4 plate.

STEP 15: Attach the tail to the body of the plane. Then place the 1 x 4 red plate across the top of the two 1 x 3 red slopes. Place the 2 x 4 red plate on top of that.

STEP 16: Turn the plane upside down and add (from front to back) two 1 x 2 inverted slopes, a 2 x 4 double inverted slope, two 1 x 2 inverted slopes, two 2 x 4 bricks and two 2 x 2 inverted slopes.

STEP 17: Add two 2 x 2 red bricks, two 2 x 2 light gray slopes and a 2 x 2 light gray brick to hold the wheels.

STEP 18: Attach the wheels as shown.

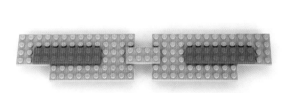

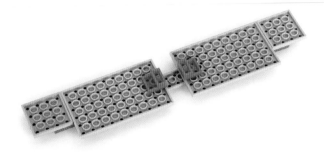

STEP 19: Build the upper wings.

STEP 20: Add two 2 x 2 red plates and two 1 x 2 red plates to the underside of the upper wings.

STEP 21: Attach the upper wings. Each side has a 1 x 2 light gray brick and a 1 x 2 light gray brick two bricks high. Or use three 1 x 2 bricks.

The plane is complete and is now ready to transport your adventurer and his sidekick on a trek around the world! Will they land the plane safely? Or will your hero end up crash landing somewhere mysterious? Or something worse?

1930s AIRPORT

Your LEGO biplane will need a classic style airport for take offs and landings! At that time, airports were not equipped with computer monitors and motorized conveyor belts to carry baggage. Build a simple airport with one main building and an air traffic control tower with windows and a radio. In the 1930s, radio was the only method of communication available to pilots and airport personnel!

KEY ELEMENTS

1—baseplate
Light gray bricks for the building
Dark gray bricks for the air traffic control tower
White bricks for the air traffic control tower

2—4 x 10 dark gray plates for the air traffic control tower
1—8 x 8 dark gray plate for the air traffic control tower
4—2 x 4 windows, 5 bricks high
1—door
2—boat windows, 2 x 8 x 2 with translucent light blue glass

5—white chairs
1—computer screen (pretend it's a radio)
1—phone, built according to the instructions in the detective office (page 88)

The roof of the airport building has been left open to make it easier to play with. Try adding slope bricks around the top edge of the building if you prefer for it to have a roof.

Create a space for passengers to sit as they wait for their flight, and build a desk for airport personnel. The phone is the same design as the desk phone in the detective office (page 88).

The air traffic control tower has space for two chairs and two minifigures to sit and monitor take-offs and landings. Use a 2 x 2 slope with a computer screen, and pretend that it's a radio rather than a computer!

CRASH LANDING AT THE PALACE RUINS

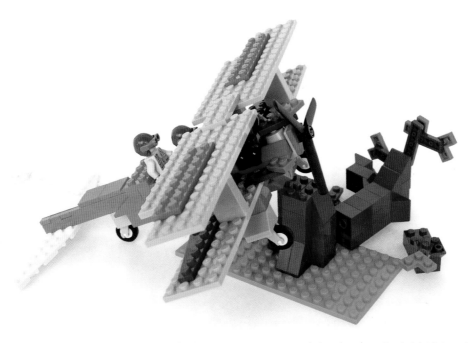

In just a few hours, Tex and Bill were within sight of the Cape. "Bill! I can't find anywhere to land!" shouted Tex above the noise of the engine. "What do you see on the map?"

"Um, I see an ocean? I don't suppose that would work. No, of course not. How about this green area? No, never mind. I think the green is hills. How about . . . um . . ."

"Bill!" shouted Tex, "Make a decision! We need to land somewhere!"

"Okay," answered Bill. "I think I've got it! Veer slightly to the right. No, the left. Well, no. Yes, actually that's right."

"Right?" Tex asked. "So I should go right?"

"No, left." yelled Bill. "It's right to go left!"

"What does that even mean!" shouted Tex, growing more exasperated by the minute.

"I should have said that's correct. Go right, I mean left." said Bill.

So Tex steered left at precisely the wrong moment, and the plane crashed right into a tree!

(continued)

Tex and Bill managed to climb down from the wrecked plane, and as they gazed around the surroundings their eyes landed on the most interesting looking building, or rather remains of a building. "Tex!" Bill exclaimed. "I think this is it! That just has to be the Palace Ruins!"

"I do believe you're right!" said Tex. "This is going to be the easiest mission ever!"

"All right, now to find this missing piece. We'll be done in five minutes!" bragged Tex.

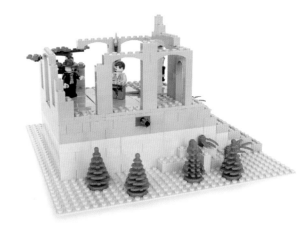

"Yikes!" screamed Bill as he stepped past a snake on the steps of the Palace Ruins.

"That's just a harmless pit viper," said Tex.

"Harmless!" shouted Bill. "That's not harmless!"

"Of course it is," said Tex. "I have a bottle of anti-venom serum in my bag. Easy cure. Snakes are no big deal to an experienced adventurer!"

Bill managed to compose himself, and they continued their search.

"I don't see anything in here at all," said Tex. "I don't even see a place where the missing piece could be hidden!"

At that moment, Bill felt himself falling. It was a trap door! "Ahhhh!" he screamed as he fell into a mysterious cavern below.

"Bill, are you okay?" Tex yelled down into the darkness.

"I'm all right!" Bill called back. "Hey, I think I found a place where something could be hidden!"

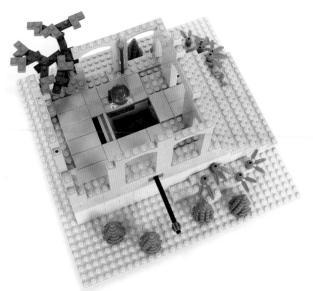

"Come on down here, Tex!" Bill called from the bottom of the cavern.

Tex was about to jump when he remembered the folding grappling hook and rope that he had in his pocket. He stuck the hook in the ground near the opening of the hole and lowered himself down with the rope.

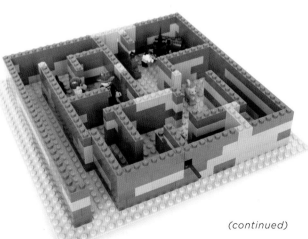

"You know what this is?" Tex said. "I think it's a massive labyrinth. A maze. The missing piece of the Crystal Bunny must be hidden here inside the labyrinth."

(continued)

Suddenly, Tex stopped dead in his tracks. "Bill," he gasped. "Look! It's . . . a . . . CAT!"

"So what?" laughed Bill. "A pit viper didn't bother you a bit, but now you're scared of this kitty cat?"

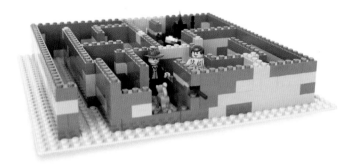

The labyrinth was Tex's worst nightmare. He was terribly (and embarrassingly) afraid of cats, and the labyrinth had meowing cats around every turn!

"Come on, Tex!" Bill pleaded. "These are just cats. Cats! Pull it together and let's move on!

Tex managed to push aside the cats (who were creepily brushing up against his legs) and pressed on through the labyrinth. Suddenly he came around a corner and saw a hideous creature wielding a deadly weapon. "Bill, I think we've got something here!" Tex yelled.

"Get back!" the creature hissed. "Who dares to disturb Oskelon and to tread upon his lair?"

Oskelon was guarding a treasure chest, and Tex knew that the missing piece just had to be inside.

Tex spotted a sword conveniently located on the wall, and grabbed it. Oskelon didn't like that either. "Don't touch the sword!" he hissed. "I'll punish you for that!"

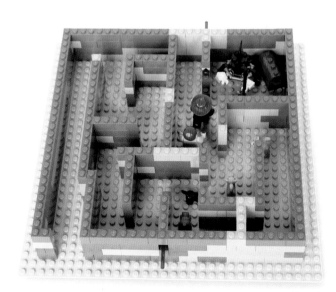

Tex valiantly fought Oskelon, persevering against the creature's brute strength. It was an epic battle!

For a moment, it looked as though Oskelon would win . . .

But Tex managed to gain the upper hand, and he chopped the creature to pieces before it had a chance to harm him with its sword.

"Hmm, this is interesting," said Tex as he examined the contents of the treasure chest. "There's a key in here. And directions to the Cliffs of Hysteria. Ugh, that doesn't exactly sound like a vacation destination! And unfortunately, I think that our missing piece is not here in this labyrinth. It has to be hidden in those cliffs, and I think we need this key to get to it. This quest is not going to be quite as easy as I thought."

(continued)

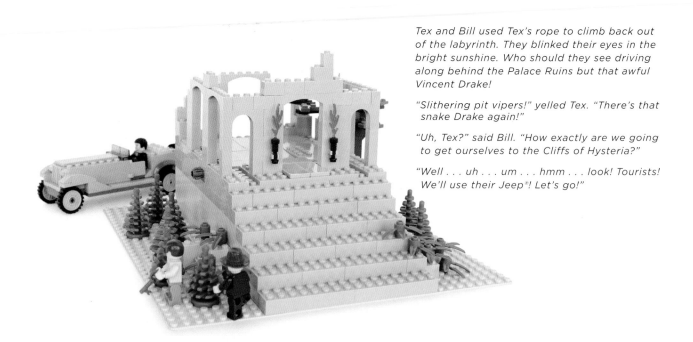

Tex and Bill used Tex's rope to climb back out of the labyrinth. They blinked their eyes in the bright sunshine. Who should they see driving along behind the Palace Ruins but that awful Vincent Drake!

"Slithering pit vipers!" yelled Tex. "There's that snake Drake again!"

"Uh, Tex?" said Bill. "How exactly are we going to get ourselves to the Cliffs of Hysteria?"

"Well . . . uh . . . um . . . hmm . . . look! Tourists! We'll use their Jeep®! Let's go!"

"Hello sir," began Tex. "That's a mighty fine Jeep you have there!"

The tourist, who was taking a picture of his wife in front of the Palace Ruins, merely grunted a reply.

Tex coughed.

"I was wondering if we could, uh, borrow that Jeep from you!"

"It's a rental," answered the man.

"Well, we can give you enough cash to rent another vehicle, plus spending money left over. Please? We really need a Jeep. As in, right now!"

The tourist started to decline Tex's offer, but then he caught sight of the wad of bills in Tex's hand. "All right, I supposed I can agree to that," he said.

"Perfect!" yelled Tex. "Come on Bill! We don't have a moment to lose!" The two adventurers jumped into the Jeep and sped away over the dusty dirt road.

THE PALACE RUINS OF CAPE CUCKOO

Construct the ruins of a mysterious ancient civilization! Make the building look as though it has crumbled after being exposed to hundreds of years of rain, sun and wind. Create a trap door that leads to a labyrinth full of danger, or invent your own adventure. Your LEGO adventurer will have an epic time exploring these ancient ruins!

KEY ELEMENTS

1—tan baseplate
Light gray arch bricks—1 x 4, 2 bricks tall
Light gray arch bricks—1 x 6
3—1 x 2 light gray bricks with a clip
1—spear
2—dark brown minifigure telescopes

2—translucent orange flames
Various light gray bricks
Various light gray plates
Various tan bricks
1—4 x 8 dark gray plate for the trap door
2—1 x 6 dark gray Technic bricks
1—1 x 2 dark gray Technic brick
1—2 x 4 light gray plate with two pins

1—Technic axle, 10 studs long
1—Technic gear, 8 tooth
Various light gray tiles
Various brown bricks and plates for the tree
2 x 2 green corner plates for tree leaves
Trees and bushes

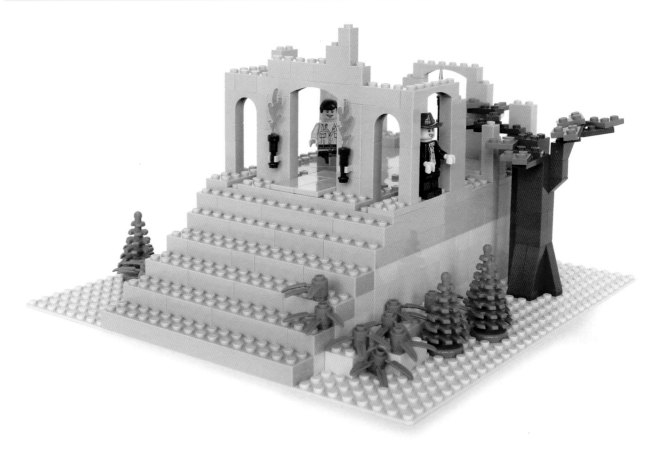

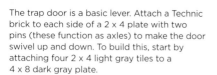

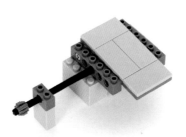

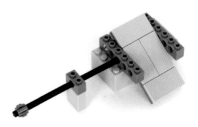

The trap door is a basic lever. Attach a Technic brick to each side of a 2 x 4 plate with two pins (these function as axles) to make the door swivel up and down. To build this, start by attaching four 2 x 4 light gray tiles to a 4 x 8 dark gray plate.

Attach the Technic bricks to the 2 x 4 plate with pins. Insert a Technic rod through a 1 x 2 Technic brick and then under the door assembly. The Technic rod should not go all the way through to the second 1 x 6 Technic brick—it stops halfway underneath the door.

To release the trap door, simply pull out the Technic rod. This allows the door to drop down.

Build the base of the Palace Ruins, and add the trap door. To conserve bricks, the inside of the base is open.

Add bricks and plates around the trap door until the level is equal with the walls of the Palace Ruins.

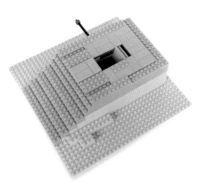

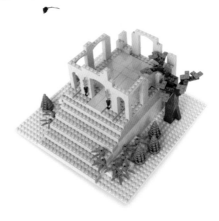

Use plates to build the floor of the Palace Ruins. Use tiles for the floor inside the building, or just use plates.

Then build walls for the Palace Ruins with bricks and arches. Use 1 x 2 bricks with a clip on the side to hold lanterns (made from a minifigure telescope and a flame) and to hang a spear on the wall. Build a tree that has grown up through the side of the building. The incomplete walls also contribute to the crumbled look of an ancient building.

DEADLY LABYRINTH

Use your LEGO bricks to construct a maze that has hidden dangers and hazards around every turn! Make the design complicated so that it will be a difficult task to get through this maze. Fill the labyrinth with vicious monsters and shooting missiles, or pretend that your hero is afraid of something silly—like cats!

KEY ELEMENTS

LABYRINTH

1—baseplate
Various gray bricks for building the walls
Spring shooter bricks with missiles
1—1 x 2 brick with a vertical clip
1—sword
Treasure chest

OSKELON THE VILLAIN CREATURE

1—2 x 2 silver plate, modified with an octagonal bar frame
1—2 x 2 black round plate
1—2 x 2 black round brick
1—1 x 2 black plate
1—2 x 2 black round plate with rounded bottom

4—black arms mechanical, ID 53989
1—black flexible spike
1—black bar
2—1 x 2 light gray plates with one clip on top
2—1 x 1 white plates with a vertical clip
2—1 x 1 translucent red round plates

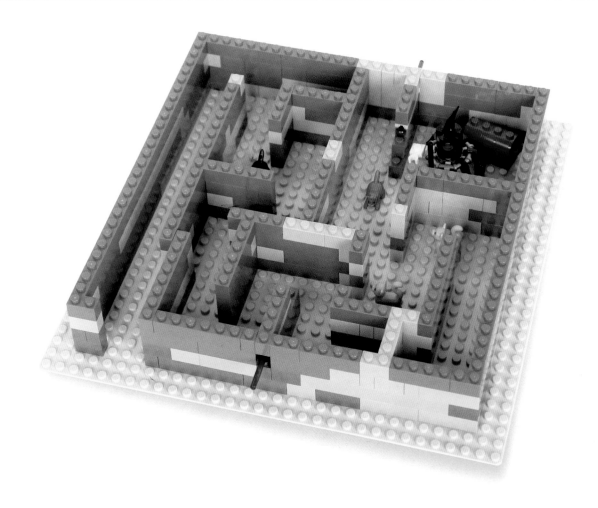

STEP 1: Build the layout for your labyrinth. Use spring shooter bricks with missiles to make the labyrinth more dangerous! Build them into the walls, leaving room to insert the missile.

STEP 2: Build the villain creature that guards the labyrinth! Gather the bricks shown.

STEP 3: Attach the black plate with the rounded bottom to the underside of the silver plate with an octagonal bar.

STEP 4: Turn the silver plate over and add the four legs.

STEP 5: Add the 2 x 2 black round brick, the two red bricks for eyes and the 1 x 2 black plate.

STEP 6: Place the 2 x 2 round plate on top of the head, and then insert the spike into the hole. Attach the white plates to the light gray plates to be arms. Attach the clip on the light gray plates to the octagonal bar. Use the black bar as a weapon. Your villain creature is now ready to defend the treasure chest with the key!

OFF-ROAD ADVENTURE JEEP®

Tex Alexander and his sidekick Bill will be ready for any adventure in this rugged Jeep, whether it's on the road or off in the wilderness. The classic style fits the setting of this adventure tale. Add clips to the back of the Jeep so that your minifigures can easily transport tools and gear.

PARTS LIST

TAN BRICKS
5—4 x 4 plates
9—1 x 6 plates
5—2 x 4 plates
7—1 x 4 plates
2—1 x 3 plates
3—1 x 2 plates
6—1 x 1 plates
5—1 x 4 bricks
1—1 x 6 brick
2—1 x 3 bricks

2—1 x 2 bricks
6—1 x 1 bricks
2—1 x 1 bricks with a stud on the side
2—1 x 2 bricks with two studs on the side
4—1 x 2 slopes, 30 degree
2—1 x 1 slopes, 30 degree
2—1 x 2 bricks with a curved top
1—2 x 2 curved slope

GRAY BRICKS
1—4 x 8 dark gray plate
2—4 x 6 dark gray plates

2—1 x 2 dark gray plates with a ladder
2—1 x 1 light gray plates with a clip
2—2 x 4 bricks with two axles

ASSORTED BRICKS
1—steering wheel
2—1 x 2 white tiles
2—1 x 2 translucent red tiles
2—1 x 2—1 x 2 black brackets, inverted
2—1 x 1 translucent yellow plates
4—large wheels
1—2 x 6 windshield
Tools (optional)

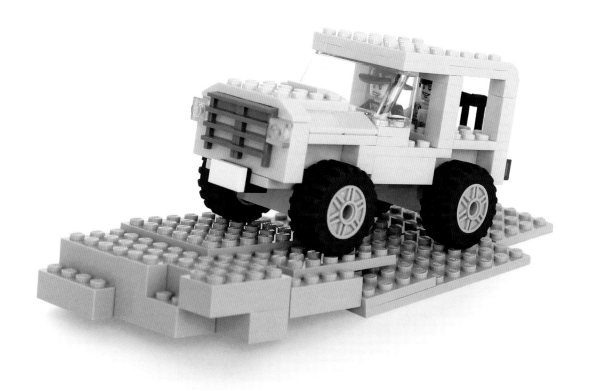

STEP 1: Start with a 2 x 4 tan plate, a 4 x 8 dark gray plate and a 4 x 4 tan plate.

STEP 2: Place two dark gray 4 x 6 plates on top of these as shown.

STEP 3: Attach a 1 x 6 tan brick on the front of the Jeep. The three bricks shown will go on the back end.

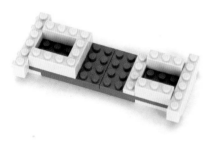

STEP 4: Attach the three bricks from step 3 to the back end of the Jeep. Then add two 1 x 4 tan bricks and a 1 x 2 tan brick to the back. Add a 1 x 4 tan plate and two 1 x 3 bricks to the front.

STEP 5: On top of the 1 x 4 plate, add a 1 x 6 tan plate and then another 1 x 4 tan plate. Then attach a 1 x 6 tan plate on each side of the Jeep. Those will be attached only at the front end at this point, but they will become more stable later.

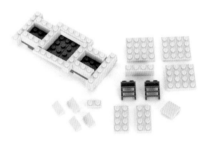

STEP 6: Gather the bricks shown for building the front end of the Jeep.

STEP 7: Place the 1 x 4 brick on the front, and attach the two 1 x 2 dark gray plates with a ladder on top of that. Then add two 2 x 4 tan plates with a 1 x 2 tan plate between them.

STEP 8: Stack two 4 x 4 tan plates and add them to the hood of the Jeep.

STEP 9: Add one more 4 x 4 tan plate so that it covers the tops of the dark gray ladders. Then add the 2 x 2 curved slope. Place two 1 x 2 slopes on each side of the hood.

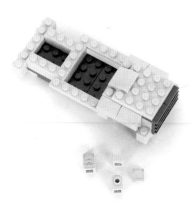

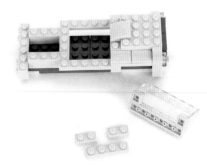

STEP 10: Attach a 1 x 1 slope to the top of a 1 x 1 brick with a stud on the side. Add a 1 x 1 translucent yellow plate as shown. Build two of these—one for each headlight.

STEP 11: Add the headlights to the Jeep. Then gather the bricks shown.

STEP 12: Attach tan plates to the underside of the windshield.

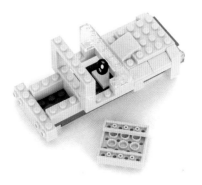

STEP 13: Add a second layer of tan plates to the underside of the windshield.

STEP 14: Attach the windshield to the Jeep and add a steering wheel.

STEP 15: Just behind the space where the driver sits, add a 1 x 6 tan plate and two 1 x 1 tan bricks on each side. Then place a 1 x 6 tan plate across those. Attach two 1 x 4 tan plates to the underside of a 4 x 4 tan plate.

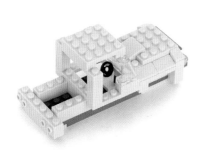

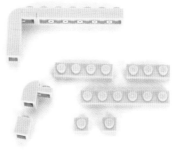

STEP 16: Place the 4 x 4 plate on top of the Jeep.

STEP 17: Attach a 1 x 6 tan plate on top of the back bumper. Then add two 2 x 4 tan plates. Attach a 1 x 4 brick on each side of the Jeep.

STEP 18: Build the two top frame sections as shown.

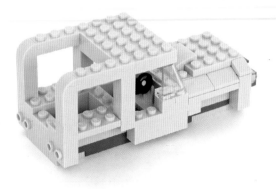

STEP 19: Attach the top frame sections to the body of the Jeep.

STEP 20: Gather two 1 x 2 translucent red tiles for the taillights. Find two 1 x 1 light gray plates with clips and some tools.

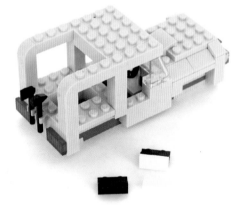

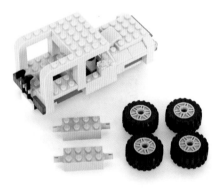

STEP 21: Add the tail lights and tools to the back of the Jeep. Then build the license plates. Attach two 1 x 2 white tiles to two 1 x 2—1 x 2 black brackets (inverted).

STEP 22: Gather four large wheels and two 2 x 4 bricks to hold the wheels.

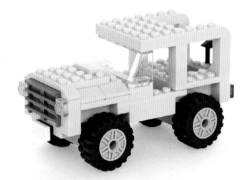

STEP 23: Attach the wheels, and the Jeep is complete!

Pretend that your minifigures are loading up their gear for an adventure! Build a river for the Jeep to cross, or some LEGO rocks for it to drive over.

SHOWDOWN AT THE CLIFFS OF HYSTERIA

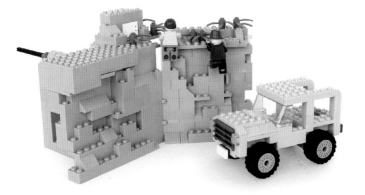

Tex and Bill rumbled through miles of dust and dirt in search of the Cliffs of Hysteria. "I think I'LL hold the map this time!" Tex yelled over the noise of the bumpy road.

It wasn't long before the pair had the sense that they were being followed. "Uh oh, Tex," said Bill. "Here comes Vincent Drake in that roadster of his, and he's catching up!"

Lucky for Tex and Bill, they soon came to a place where a bubbling creek crossed the dirt road. The Jeep rumbled through the water with no problem at all, but Drake's wheels sank into the water and stuck fast in the mud.

"This must be the cliffs!" shouted Tex as they came around a bend in the road. Tex quickly parked the Jeep, and he and Bill began scrambling up the side of the cliffs.

"Ah ha!" said Tex. "Here it is! This little box must hold the missing piece to the Crystal Bunny! Quick, hand me the key."

"Um, I don't have it," Bill said a little sheepishly. "I must have left it in the Jeep!"

"Well, get down there and get it!" Tex yelled.

(continued)

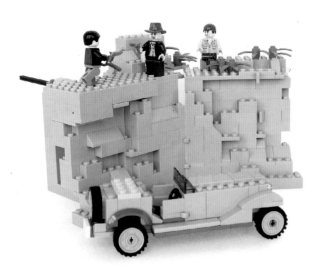

But as it turns out, Bill didn't have to get the key because at that moment they both turned around to see Vincent Drake with the key in one hand and a pistol in the other!

"All right," Drake said in a voice so calm it was scary. "Step away from the box, let me get the missing piece of the Crystal Bunny, and no one gets hurt."

Someone did get hurt, however. At the moment that he made his threat, the rocks at the edge of the cliffs crumbled, and Drake fell to the ground below! Quick as a flash, Bill seized his chance and scrambled down for the key.

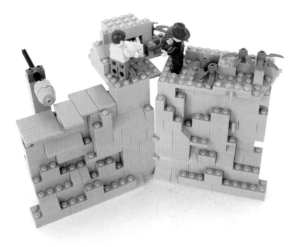

With the key safely in hand, Tex opened the box and pulled out the missing piece of the Crystal Bunny. At last!

"What part of the bunny could this possibly be?" Bill wondered.

"Who knows?" Tex replied. "But let's get back to the museum! I want my reward money!"

ROADSTER

The roadster is a classic car design that features an open top and two seats. This 1930s style roadster is the perfect vehicle for villain Vincent Drake to drive as he zooms around town and chases Tex and Bill! As awesome as this car looks, however, it's not built for off-road adventures. Build a scene where Drake gets stuck in a river!

PARTS LIST

LIGHT GRAY BRICKS
2—2 x 4 plates
8—1 x 2 plates
2—2 x 6 bricks
2—2 x 4 bricks
3—1 x 4 bricks
2—1 x 2 bricks
4—1 x 1 bricks
2—1 x 3 slopes
2—1 x 1 bricks with a stud on the side
2—1 x 1 bricks with a stud on the side (headlight)
1—2 x 4 tile
2—1 x 6 tiles
2—1 x 2 tiles

1—2 x 2 tile
4—1 x 2 grills
2—1 x 3 curved slopes
6—1 x 1 slopes, 30 degree
2—1 x 2—1 x 2 hinge plates
2—1 x 2 x 1 panels
2—1 x 1 panels, corner
1—1 x 2 brick with two studs on the side
2—2 x 4 plates with two pins
2—2 x 2 plates with one stud on top

DARK GRAY BRICKS
1—6 x 6 plate
1—4 x 10 plate
1—4 x 6 plate
1—2 x 6 plate
1—1 x 6 plate

2—1 x 4 plates
4 x 2½ x 1⅔ vehicle mudguards with arch
1—1 x 2—1 x 2 bracket, inverted

TAN BRICKS
1—2 x 4 plate
1—1 x 2—2 x 2 bracket
1—1 x 2 tile
1—1 x 2 slope, 30 degree

ASSORTED BRICKS
1—1 x 2 white tile
2—1 x 2 x 1 translucent black panels
2—1 x 1 clear round plates
1—steering wheel
5—wheels

STEP 1: Find a 4 x 6 dark gray plate and a 4 x 10 dark gray plate.

STEP 2: Flip them upside down and add (from left to right) a 2 x 4 light gray plate, a 2 x 4 plate with two pins, a 1 x 4 dark gray plate, a 1 x 6 dark gray plate, a 2 x 6 dark gray plate, a 6 x 6 dark gray plate, a 1 x 4 dark gray plate and one more 2 x 4 plate with two pins.

STEP 3: Turn the car over again and add two 1 x 6 tiles, two 1 x 3 slopes, two 1 x 1 corner panels and a 1 x 2 tile.

STEP 4: Add two 2 x 6 bricks and two 1 x 2 plates.

STEP 5: Attach a 1 x 2 brick with two studs on the side and two 1 x 1 bricks with a stud on the side (headlight). Add a 1 x 2 tile.

STEP 6: Add a 1 x 4 brick and two 2 x 4 bricks just behind the headlights.

STEP 7: Place a 1 x 2 grill and a 1 x 1 slope on each side of the car. Then gather the bricks shown.

STEP 8: Add one hinge plate on each side of the car. The grill bricks underneath will allow the door to swing open and closed.

STEP 9: Place a 1 x 2 brick on each side of the car. Then add a 2 x 4 plate on top of those.

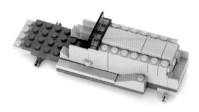

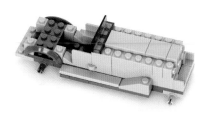

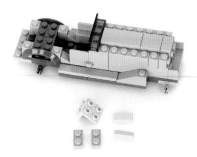

STEP 10: Add the panels for the doors and the windshield, and then place the tiles on the hood of the car.

STEP 11: Add two 2 x 2 dark gray mudguards and four 1 x 1 light gray bricks.

STEP 12: Gather the bricks shown for building the seat of the roadster.

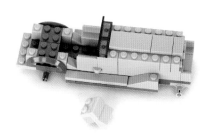

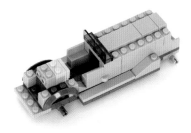

STEP 13: Stack the two 1 x 2 light gray plates and attach them under the tan bracket.

STEP 14: Attach the 1 x 2 tile and the 1 x 2 slope to the bracket.

STEP 15: Attach the seat to the car so that it covers the front two studs of the wheel arches. Then add two 1 x 1 light gray bricks with a stud on the side.

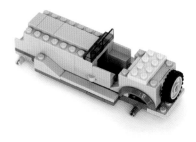

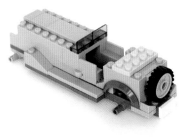

STEP 16: Stack two 1 x 2 light gray plates and attach them to the back of the car. Then find a 2 x 2 plate with one stud on top and a wheel.

STEP 17: Attach the wheel to the 2 x 2 plate and add that to the back of the car. Place a 1 x 4 brick on either side above the wheel arch, and then add a 2 x 4 tan plate to the top of the seat area.

STEP 18: Add two 1 x 1 light gray slopes to the back of the car. Build a license plate by attaching a 1 x 2 tile to a 1 x 2—1 x 2 dark gray inverted bracket. Attach this to the underside of the car.

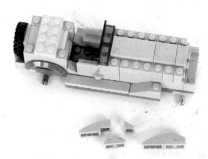

STEP 19: Build the two front fenders as shown. Each one has a 1 x 3 curved slope, a 1 x 2 plate and a 1 x 1 slope.

STEP 20: Gather the bricks shown for the steering wheel, headlights and wheels.

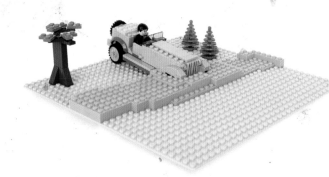

STEP 21: Attach the grills and headlights to the front of the car. Add wheels, and the roadster is complete!

Now your adventure story villain is ready to screech through the streets of town in his stylish roadster! Pretend that he is hot on the heels of the hero trying to get the key to the Cliffs of Hysteria, or build a river for him to get stuck in.

Make it look like the roadster is stuck in the water by removing the front wheels. Build the river, but leave a space the size of the car. When you put the car in the space it will look like the water is coming up around the wheels.

CLIFFS OF HYSTERIA

These dangerous cliffs provide the perfect place for a showdown with the bad guy! Use a combination of bricks and slopes to make the cliffs look like real rocks. Build them with a fun feature—a sliding LEGO hammer causes the top of the cliffs to crumble away, sending the bad guy to his doom. After all, they aren't called the Cliffs of Hysteria for nothing!

KEY ELEMENTS

Various light gray bricks and slopes
Various light gray plates
2—1 x 2—1 x 2 light gray hinge plates

1—2 x 3 x 2 container for holding the missing piece of the Crystal Bunny
1—Technic axle, 10 studs long
1—2 x 2 light gray round brick with an x-shaped hole

1—2 x 2 light gray cone, truncated
4—2 x 4 light gray tiles
Trees and plants

Use hinge plates to build the cliffs in two sections that can swivel. This makes them much more interesting than just a flat wall. Each time you add a hinge plate, you'll need to add an entire layer of plates to keep things level. Another option is to use hinge bricks, if you have them, or to stack two 1 x 2 plates on each side of the hinge plate to make it the same height as a brick.

As you build upwards, use a variety of bricks and slopes to give the cliffs some texture. Add in some bricks with a handle on the side for minifigures to use as hand holds while they climb.

At the top of the cliffs, attach the 2 x 3 container with bricks surrounding it so that it appears hidden in the rocks. Add plants. It would also be fun to hide a LEGO snake among the rocks!

Build an arm on the back of the cliffs that can hold the hammer. Slide a 2 x 2 round brick and a 2 x 2 truncated cone onto a black axle. Then slide this through a Technic brick to hold it. Build two sections of rock that are simply resting on top of tiles. They should not be attached to the cliffs in any way.

Push the hammer forward, and the cliffs begin to crumble!

And now the rocks have tumbled to the ground! Now you're ready to build a chase scene with your minifigure heroes and villains! Who will come out on top? Hopefully it's the good guy!

THE CRYSTAL BUNNY REVEALED!

"Here you go, Dr. Cooper. We've found the missing piece of the Crystal Bunny! Or, missing pieces I guess. We have no idea what these are!" said Bill.

"Excellent, men!" Dr. Cooper exclaimed. "Did you encounter any trouble?"

"Not much," Tex replied. "Nothing that two men of adventure couldn't handle!"

Everyone waited with bated breath as the museum conservator carefully added the pieces to the statue. Then he turned the statue around for all to see.

"It's breathtaking!" gasped Dr. Cooper while Tex and Bill held back laughter. They had traveled all that way to find the missing teeth of a cross-eyed, buck-toothed statue that resembled a giant chocolate bunny!

"Thank you both for your contribution to this grand museum exhibit," said Dr. Cooper as he handed Tex the cash.

"It's no problem at all," Tex responded. "Well, there's another adventure for the books, eh, Bill?"

CRYSTAL BUNNY

This silly museum statue has a comical look with its crossed eyes and large front teeth! Build a platform for the statue to sit on, and display it with pride in your LEGO museum. After all, this is a world famous statue, worth millions of LEGO dollars!

PARTS LIST

BROWN BRICKS
4—2 x 4 plates
4—1 x 4 plates
1—2 x 2 plate
2—1 x 3 plates
1—2 x 6 brick

3—2 x 4 bricks
2—1 x 4 bricks
4—1 x 2 bricks
2—1 x 1 bricks
2—1 x 1 bricks with a stud on the side (headlight)
6—1 x 1 bricks with a stud on the side
2—2 x 2 slopes

2—1 x 2 slopes, 30 degree
1—1 x 2 plate with one stud on top

ASSORTED BRICKS
2—1 x 1 white plates with one claw
2—eyes
1—1 x 1 round pink plate

STEP 1: Build the feet of the bunny. Each foot has a 2 x 2 slope, a 1 x 2 brick and a 1 x 2 slope (30 degree).

STEP 2: Connect the feet with a 2 x 4 plate.

STEP 3: Add three 2 x 4 bricks.

STEP 4: Build the arms by attaching a 1 x 4 plate to each side of a 2 x 6 brick.

STEP 5: Add a 2 x 4 plate and a 1 x 4 plate to the top of the body.

STEP 6: Stack two 1 x 4 bricks on the back of the head. Then add two 1 x 1 bricks and two 1 x 1 bricks with a stud on the side.

STEP 7: Add a 2 x 4 plate, a 1 x 4 plate and two 1 x 1 bricks with a stud on the side (headlight).

STEP 8: Attach a 1 x 2 plate with one stud on top to the headlight bricks from the previous step and add a 1 x 1 pink round plate for the nose. Add the eyes, and turn them so that they are crossed for a silly look! The eyes are attached to 1 x 1 bricks with a stud on the side, and there is a 1 x 2 brick between the eyes.

STEP 9: Turn the bunny around and add a 1 x 2 brick and two 1 x 1 bricks with a stud on the side. Attach two 1 x 3 plates to these to be the ears.

STEP 10: Add a 2 x 4 plate and a 2 x 2 plate to the top of the bunny's head. Make the bunny teeth with two 1 x 1 one plates with one claw. The bunny is now complete!

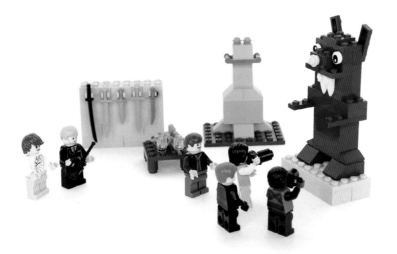

Create other exhibits such as a sword display, creative statues and a table full of jewels. The Crystal Bunny will be the main attraction with visitors coming from around the world! Well, until someone notices just how goofy that bunny looks!

THE BEST WORST CAMPING TRIP EVER

Use your LEGO bricks to create a wilderness adventure! Build a campsite with a tent, picnic table and cooler. Then load up your minifigure family into their sporty SUV full of gear. It's going to be the most awesome week of camping ever! Or is it? The car catches on fire, Dad accidentally crashes into the campground's souvenir and bait shop and bears ransack the campsite. It might not be the best camping trip, but it's definitely the best *worst* camping trip ever!

MARSHMALLOWS ON FIRE

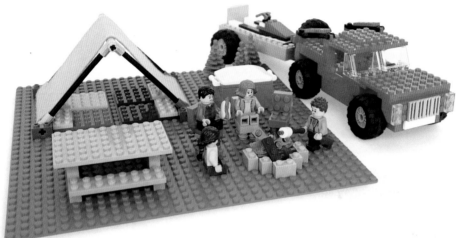

After a very hectic end to the school year, the Jones family was thrilled to be on summer vacation at last! "This is going to be an amazing week!" Dad said as he fixed himself another hot dog. "Nothing but campfires and relaxing on the lake!"

"No cleaning or laundry or grocery shopping!" said Mom. "I am so ready for a week of fun!"

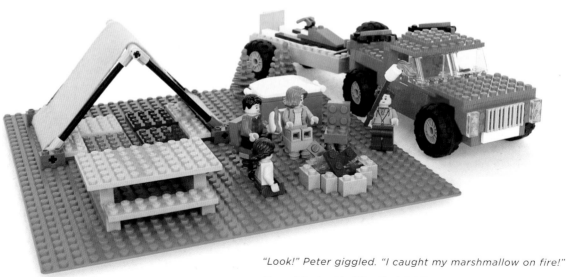

"Look!" Peter giggled. "I caught my marshmallow on fire!"

"I want to try that!" yelled Addie.

"Hmm," said Dad. "Just be careful. You're getting awfully close to the car with that burning marshmallow!"

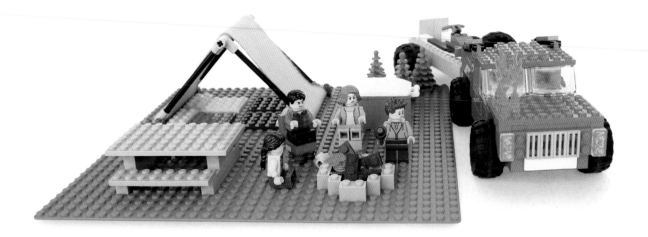

But at that moment, Peter was making another big flourish with his burning marshmallow in the air, and the stick flipped out of his hand and landed on the hood of the SUV. The front of the vehicle went up in flames!

Dad jumped to his feet and grabbed the fire extinguisher. It's always good to be prepared while camping! In no time, he had the fire out . . .

. . . but the front of the family's SUV was scorched!

"Don't worry, honey," Mom said. "Let's not let this spoil our vacation! We'll take it to the body shop when we get back home."

COZY CAMPSITE

Build a campsite complete with a minifigure-sized tent, picnic table, cooler and campfire! There are even camp chairs for sitting and relaxing by the fire. A simple piece of felt turns a pile of bricks into an adorable tent that holds four LEGO sleeping bags. Use 1 x 1 white round bricks to be marshmallows. Just make sure they don't get close to anything if they catch on fire!

PARTS LIST

TENT

4—Technic axles, 10 studs long
3—Technic axles, 12 studs long
4—1 x 2 dark gray Technic bricks with an x-shaped axle hole
2—light gray Technic axle and pin connectors, #6, 90 degrees
4—light or dark gray Technic axle and pin connectors, #1
2—light gray Technic bush
2—light gray Technic bush, ½ length
1—piece of felt, 2½ inches by 9½ inches (6 × 24 cm)
Glue—hot glue or other glue suitable for fabric

SLEEPING BAGS

4 x 6 plates, any color
2 x 4 plates, any color

PICNIC TABLE

1—6 x 10 plate
2—1 x 8 bricks
2—1 x 4 bricks
2—1 x 4 plates
2—2 x 8 plates

COOLER

2—2 x 6 blue plates
1—1 x 4 blue plate
1—1 x 2 blue plate
2—1 x 6 blue bricks
4—1 x 4 blue bricks
2—1 x 2 blue bricks
1—1 x 4 blue tile
1—1 x 2 blue tile
2—1 x 2 white plates with a handle on the side
1—white wedge, 6 x 4 x ⅔, quad curved

CAMP CHAIR

1—1 x 2 light gray plate with a handle on the side, free ends
1—1 x 2 light gray plate with one horizontal clip on the side
8—1 x 1 light gray round plates
2—2 x 4 plates, any color
2—1 x 2 plates, any color

CAMPFIRE

4—1 x 2 light gray bricks
4—1 x 1 light gray bricks
2—1 x 3 brown plates
2—1 x 4 brown plates
Fire accessory bricks
1 x 1 white round bricks for marshmallows
1—brown bar, 6 studs long for a marshmallow toasting stick

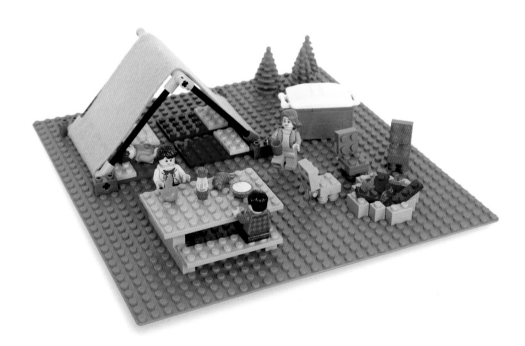

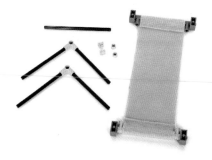

TENT

STEP 1: Gather the bricks shown for building the tent. Cut a piece of felt so that it measures 2½ inches by 9½ inches (6 × 24 cm). Fold up each end to create a pocket for a Technic axle. Check to make sure that a Technic axle will fit through the pocket and then glue it.

STEP 2: Insert the four Technic axles (10 studs long) into the two 90 degree Technic connectors.

STEP 3: Insert a Technic axle (12 studs long) into each of the pockets in the felt. Place a Technic connector and a 1 x 2 Technic brick with an x-shaped axle hole on each of the four ends. The Technic bricks will fit snugly, but the Technic connector pieces will spin freely.

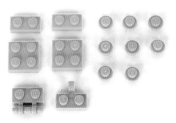

STEP 4: Insert the two 90 degree Technic connectors with the axles attached into the Technic connectors (type #1). Put a Technic bush on each side of the 90 degree Technic connectors to hold them in place along the axle.

STEP 5: The completed tent should look like this. Attach the four 1 x 2 Technic bricks to a baseplate to make it part of the camp site.

CAMP CHAIR

STEP 1: Gather the bricks shown for building the camp chair.

STEP 2: Attach the two light gray plates. Line them up with the 1 x 2 lime green plates as shown.

STEP 3: Place a 2 x 2 plate on each side to attach the bricks from the previous step. Make stacks with two 1 x 1 round plates each to be the legs.

STEP 4: Add the legs to the chair. Now your minifigures are ready to sit by the fire and toast (burn?) some marshmallows!

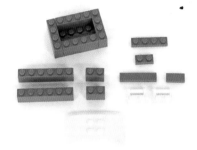

COOLER

STEP 1: Gather the bricks shown to build the cooler. Make it blue, or choose another color!

STEP 2: Attach four 1 x 4 bricks to the two 2 x 6 plates as shown.

STEP 3: Add another layer of bricks.

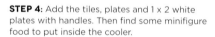

STEP 4: Add the tiles, plates and 1 x 2 white plates with handles. Then find some minifigure food to put inside the cooler.

STEP 5: Use a 6 x 4 x ⅔ wedge with four curved sides as a lid. The completed cooler is so cute!

PICNIC TABLE

Use two 1 x 8 bricks as the base of the table. Each side has a 1 x 4 brick with a 1 x 4 plate on top. Then use 2 x 8 plates for the benches and a 6 x 10 plate for the top of the table. Use three 1 x 1 red round bricks and a 1 x 1 translucent yellow cone to make a camping lantern.

CAMPFIRE

Build a campfire ring with four 1 x 2 bricks and four 1 x 1 bricks. Use brown plates to be logs, and then add fire pieces. Now your minifigures are all set for camping!

RUGGED RED SUV

This awesome SUV is especially fun because two minifigures can sit up front. With the space in the back, your minifigures can either load up plenty of camping gear or fit in two more minifigures for a ride. There is a trailer hitch on the back for pulling a trailer with a Jet Ski®, or whatever you want to build. Now it's time to head to the campground!

PARTS LIST

RED BRICKS
1—4 x 12 plate
1—6 x 6 plate
2—4 x 8 plates
3—2 x 8 plates
7—2 x 6 plates
1—1 x 8 plate
5—1 x 6 plates
9—1 x 4 plates
7—1 x 2 plates
1—4 x 4 plate
3—2 x 2 plates
1—2 x 8 brick
1—1 x 8 brick
5—1 x 6 bricks
2—2 x 4 bricks
2—2 x 3 bricks
2—2 x 2 bricks
7—1 x 2 bricks

4—1 x 4 bricks
2—1 x 3 bricks
8—1 x 1 bricks
2—1 x 4 bricks with 4 studs on the side
2—1 x 2 inverted slopes
2—2 x 2 tiles
1—1 x 2 tile
1—1 x 1 tile
3—1 x 4 tiles
1—1 x 1 plate
2—1 x 1 bricks with a stud on the side
4—1 x 1 plates with a vertical clip
1—1 x 2—2 x 2 bracket
1—car door, right
1—car door, left
1—1 x 2 plate with a handle on the side
1—1 x 2 plate with two clips on the side
2—1 x 1 plates with a clip on top
2—1 x 2 grills

GRAY BRICKS
1—4 x 10 dark gray plate
2—1 x 2 dark gray plates
4—1 x 2 light gray grills
1—1 x 4 light gray plate with a socket, flattened with holes
1—2 x 2 dark gray plate with an axle pin

ASSORTED BRICKS
4—1 x 2 white bricks with a pin
4—1 x 2 black plates with a handle on the end
1—1 x 4 white tile
2—1 x 2 translucent yellow plates
2—1 x 1 black plates with a horizontal clip
2—1 x 1 translucent red round plates
5—wheels
1—steering wheel
2—2 x 4 windshields
Assorted bricks for the engine components

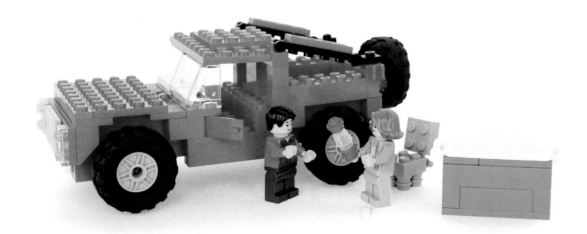

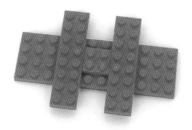

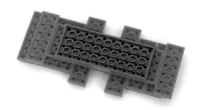

STEP 1: Place two 2 x 8 plates and a 2 x 2 plate on top of a 4 x 12 plate as shown.

STEP 2: Add a 6 x 6 plate and two 2 x 6 plates.

STEP 3: Turn the SUV over and add two 2 x 6 plates and a dark gray 4 x 10 plate.

STEP 4: Stack a 1 x 6 red plate on top of a 1 x 4 red plate. Do this a total of four times. Then add them to the underside of the vehicle next to the gray plate as shown.

STEP 5: Turn the vehicle back over. Attach a 1 x 2 plate and a 1 x 4 plate to the bottom of a 2 x 6 plate.

STEP 6: Turn it over and add it to the right side of the vehicle as shown.

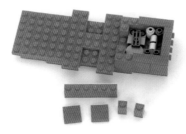

STEP 7: Add two 1 x 4 bricks, two 1 x 2 bricks and a 1 x 4 brick with four studs on the side.

STEP 8: Add three 1 x 4 tiles and two 1 x 1 bricks. Then add round bricks and plates to create engine components. Find a 1 x 6 brick, two 1 x 1 bricks and two 2 x 2 tiles.

STEP 9: Place the 1 x 6 brick and the two 1 x 1 bricks just behind the engine. Then add the 2 x 2 red tiles.

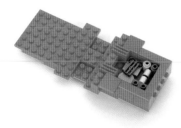

STEP 10: Add two 1 x 2 grills.

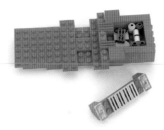

STEP 11: Build the front grill. Attach two 1 x 2 translucent yellow plates, four 1 x 2 light gray grills and two 1 x 2 inverted slopes to a 2 x 8 plate.

STEP 12: Attach the grill to the front of the SUV.

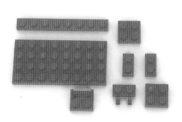

STEP 13: Gather the bricks shown for building the hood of the SUV.

STEP 14: Assemble the hood as shown.

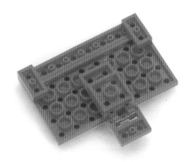

STEP 15: Attach the 1 x 2 plate with a handle on the side to the 1 x 2 plate with clips on the side. Add the 2 x 2 plate for added stability. This joint will allow the hood to open and close.

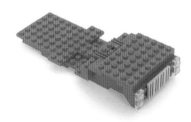

STEP 16: Put the hood in place by attaching the 1 x 2 plate with a handle on the side to the vehicle.

STEP 17: Install the steering wheel and a door on each side. Add a 1 x 2 brick next to the steering wheel.

STEP 18: Stabilize the car doors by adding a 1 x 2 plate on each side connecting the door with the frame. Add a 1 x 2 tile and a 1 x 1 tile to the dashboard.

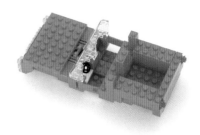

STEP 19: Add a 2 x 8 brick, four 1 x 1 bricks, two 1 x 2 bricks and two 2 x 4 windshields.

STEP 20: Build the back of the SUV. Add a 1 x 8 brick, a 1 x 6 brick, two 1 x 4 bricks, two 1 x 2 bricks and two 1 x 1 bricks with a stud on the side (headlight). Attach 1 x 1 translucent red round plates for the tail lights. Then find the bricks shown.

STEP 21: Attach the two 2 x 3 bricks and the two 2 x 2 bricks as shown.

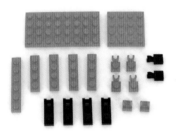

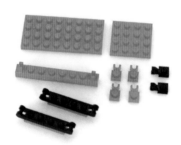

STEP 22: Gather the bricks shown for building the roof and angled sections of the frame.

STEP 23: Attach two 1 x 2 black plates with a handle on the end to a 1 x 4 red plate. Make two of these. Then attach a 1 x 6 red plate and two 1 x 1 red plates with a clip on the top to two 1 x 4 red plates.

STEP 24: Use a 4 x 4 red plate to attach the stacked plates from Step 23 to a 4 x 8 red plate.

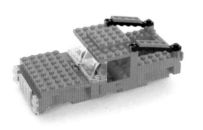

STEP 25: Stack two 1 x 1 red plates with a vertical clip and a 1 x 1 black plate with a horizontal clip, and then make a second one. Then assemble the frame as shown.

STEP 26 Attach the roof to the SUV.

STEP 27: Place a 1 x 2 red plate on top of a 1 x 6 brick. Make two of these.

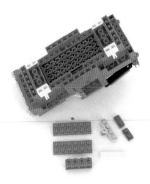

STEP 28: Attach one on each side of the SUV just under the door.

STEP 29: Turn the SUV upside down. Add four 1 x 2 white bricks with a pin and two 2 x 4 red bricks. Then add a 1 x 6 red brick or two 1 x 3 red bricks on each end.

STEP 30: Gather the bricks shown for building the license plate and the trailer hitch.

STEP 31: Attach the 1 x 4 white tile to the 1 x 4 brick with four studs on the side. Place the 1 x 2 dark gray plates on top of the 1 x 4 plate with a socket.

STEP 32: Attach the license plate in the front and the trailer hitch to the back. Place a 2 x 6 plate over each end so that it covers the white bricks.

STEP 33: Add the wheels, and then build the spare tire. Find a 1 x 2–2 x 2 bracket, a 2 x 2 plate with a pin on top and a wheel.

STEP 34: Attach the 2 x 2 plate with the axle pin to the bracket and attach those to the SUV as shown.

STEP 35: Install the spare tire, and the SUV is complete!

Make the SUV look like it was burned in a fire! Replace some of the red bricks with black bricks. Give the grill a crooked look by placing a 1 x 1 black plate under one of the grill bricks.

WATCH OUT FOR THAT DEER!

Early the next morning, the family decided to head out to find the campground's store and bait shop.

"Look! I see the store up ahead!" Peter yelled.

"Oh! Watch out for that deer!" Mom yelled.

"The store is on the left! Do you see it, Dad?" Peter called.

Dad swerved to the left to avoid the deer and crashed right into the store!

"AHHH!" screamed the kids from the back seat.

"Sweetie, WHAT are you doing!" yelled Mom.

A very surprised (and upset!) store owner came running out to see what had happened.

"Hey, what in the world is going on out here?" he asked.

Dad sighed before saying, "I'm sorry, I was trying to avoid hitting a deer and hit your store instead."

"I'll say!" replied the store owner.

After discussing insurance policies with the now slightly calmer store owner, the family surveyed the damage done to their SUV.

"This is great, Dad!" said Peter.

"Great?" asked Dad.

"Yeah!" Peter replied. "Now we can buy the new Land Master DX-63! Have you seen it? The suspension is AWESOME!"

"Cars cost money, son," Dad answered through gritted teeth. "I don't want the Land Master DX-63! I want this car to be NOT BANGED UP!"

"It's okay, honey," Mom said. "Let's try to just enjoy the rest of our vacation!"

CAMPGROUND STORE AND BAIT SHOP

Build a camp store with firewood, bait and supplies for sale! This building has a fun twist. Some of the bricks are resting in place but are not connected to the building. Crash a LEGO car into the side of the building and the wall crumbles! Oops!

KEY ELEMENTS

1—tan baseplate
Various dark gray bricks
Dark gray tiles for creating the trick section of the wall
4—1 x 4 windows, 3 bricks high
1—1 x 4 door, 6 bricks high

2 x 4 and 2 x 2 dark blue slopes for the roof, or use any color
6—Various tan plates and bricks for building the store shelves
2 x 4 light gray tiles for the shop counter and the front walkway
1 x 1 round bricks in various translucent colors

1 x 1 round plates in various colors
Dark gray 1 x 1 round tiles
1—4 x 4 dark gray plate
1—2 x 2 dark gray plate
Gray panels, 1 x 2 x 1 and 1 x 1, corner
2 x 6 brown plates for flower beds
Various flowers and plants
1 x 3 brown plates for firewood

The building looks solid, but that is a trick!

When building your store, leave a gap in the walls. Making the gap an uneven shape will make the damage seem more natural. Add a row of tiles around the bottom of the gap. Then create bricks with smooth tops to fit inside the gap.

It takes three plates (or tiles) to equal the height of one brick. If you leave a four brick high gap, you can fill it with three of these bricks sections. Create two layers that consist of one brick with a tile on top, and then for the final layer use two plates stacked with a tile on top.

Build a counter inside the store, and shelves for supplies.

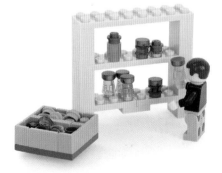

Build a display shelf and fill it with bottles built from 1 x 1 round bricks or cones with a 1 x 1 round tile on top for a lid. For the bin, place a 4 x 4 plate on top of a 2 x 2 plate. Then use panels to create the sections of the bin.

Oh no, the SUV definitely has some damage from that crash! Oops!

Make one of the front wheels sit at a funny angle by replacing the bricks around the wheel with the bricks shown.

Attach a 1 x 2 Technic brick to the wheel using a light gray pin.

Attach the 1 x 2 hinge plate with two fingers to the 1 x 2 hinge plate with one finger. These will allow the wheel to tilt and look broken! Attach one plate under the Technic brick that holds the wheel, and place a 1 x 2 brick on top of the other.

Attach the new wheel assembly to the SUV.

...ce the two dark gray plates to the left of the wheel. Then use the ...x 4 red plate to hold it all together.

Oh boy! Look at that mangled SUV! The hinge plates allow you to position the wheel at the angle you want, and then they lock in place. Remove a few bricks from the front of the car to contribute to the banged up look.

DEER

Build a LEGO deer to add to your LEGO wilderness, or build several! This woodland creature is perfect to go with your camping scene. Just make sure that your minifigures know to watch for deer while driving on the road! Swerving might just be a bad idea!

PARTS LIST

BROWN BRICKS
4—2 x 4 plates
1—2 x 3 plate
1—2 x 2 plate
4—1 x 2 plates
4—1 x 3 plates
2—1 x 2 plates with one stud on top

2—2 x 4 bricks
14—1 x 2 bricks
2—2 x 2 slopes, inverted
4—1 x 2 slopes
6—1 x 2 slopes, 30 degree
2—1 x 1 slopes, 30 degree
4—1 x 1 bricks
2—1 x 1 bricks with a stud on the side

TAN BRICKS
4—2 x 4 plates
2—1 x 3 plates
1—2 x 2 plate
4—1 x 2 plates

ASSORTED BRICKS
2—1 x 2 black plates
2—eyes

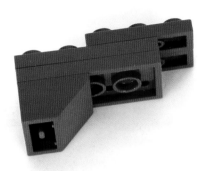

STEP 1: Build the head of the deer. Start with a 2 x 2 inverted slope, two 2 x 4 plates and two 1 x 3 plates.

STEP 2: Add two 1 x 2 black plates for the nose. Then add two 1 x 1 bricks with a stud on the side, two eyes and a 1 x 2 brick.

STEP 3: Place two 1 x 1 slopes in front of the eyes. Then add a 1 x 2 plate and a 1 x 2 plate with one stud on top.

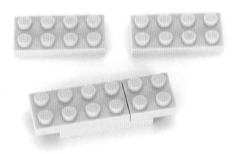

STEP 4: Build the body of the deer. Attach a 2 x 4 tan plate and a 2 x 2 tan plate on top of a 2 x 4 tan plate.

STEP 5: Add two 2 x 4 tan plates on top.

STEP 6: From left to right, add a 2 x 4 plate, a 2 x 3 plate, another 2 x 4 plate and a 2 x 2 inverted slope.

STEP 7: Add two 2 x 4 bricks and a 1 x 2 plate.

STEP 8: Attach the deer's head to his body. Add a 2 x 2 plate and a 1 x 2 plate on the deer's back just behind the head.

STEP 9: Add a 1 x 2 brick, a 1 x 2 plate and a 1 x 2 slope behind the head. Then add another 1 x 2 slope behind the neck. Build the legs. Each leg has a 1 x 2 slope, a 1 x 1 brick and three 1 x 2 bricks. Then gather the bricks shown.

STEP 10: Place a 1 x 2 plate with one stud on top on the back of the deer. Attach a 1 x 3 plate for the tail. Attach two 1 x 2 tan plates under the rear. Place a 1 x 2 slope at the top of each leg.

STEP 11: Build the antlers with the remaining plates and attach them to the 1 x 2 plate with one stud on top, on top of the head. The deer is complete! Build a forest for your deer, or pretend that he is venturing out on the road. Just don't let him get hit by a car!

DISASTER ON THE LAKE

After spending an unpleasant morning on the phone with an insurance adjuster, everyone decided that it was high time to head to the lake!

In no time at all, Dad and Addie were zipping through the water while Peter patiently waited his turn on the shore.

"Is it my turn yet?" Peter called.

"Just a minute!" Addie called back. "Let me finish my turn! I just got on it!"

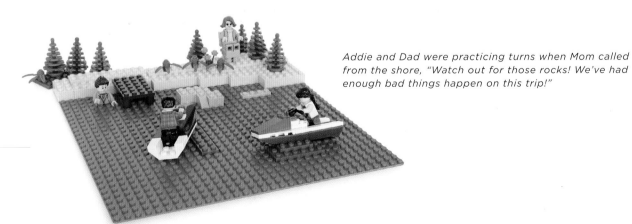

Addie and Dad were practicing turns when Mom called from the shore, "Watch out for those rocks! We've had enough bad things happen on this trip!"

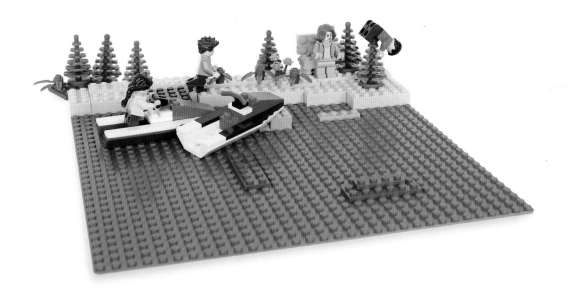

Unfortunately, Dad was going way too fast, didn't see the rocks and wouldn't have been able to make an adjustment in steering even if he had heard what Mom said! His Jet Ski slammed into the rocks and he flew over the handlebars and into a tree!

"Ow," Dad groaned as Mom came running to help.

"Come on kids!" sighed Mom. "Looks like we're headed to the emergency room!"

The emergency clinic got Dad's broken leg all bandaged up, although the doctor did tell him that he had to stay off his feet completely until he was able to have a follow-up x-ray with his doctor at home. This was pretty much the last thing Dad wanted to hear on vacation!

JET SKI® AND TRAILER

Give your minifigures a day of fun in the water by building them a LEGO lake complete with a dock and some Jet Skis to ride! Create a simple trailer that attaches to the back of the SUV, and transporting the Jet Skis to the lake will be a breeze. It's a day of summer relaxation! Well, until disaster strikes, that is! Watch out for those rocks!

PARTS LIST

JET SKI
1—4 x 4 white double slope, inverted
1—6 x 4 white wedge, inverted
2—1 x 4 dark blue tiles
1—4 x 4 dark blue wedge plate
1—1 x 2 red plate
1—2 x 4 red brick
1—2 x 4 red slope
1—1 x 1 black plate with a clip on top
2—1 x 2 white tiles
1—1 x 2 white plate with one stud on top
1—handlebars

TRAILER
2—6 x 6 light gray plates
1—2 x 4 light gray plate
1—2 x 3 light gray plate
1—2 x 14 light gray plate
5—1 x 6 light gray bricks
1—2 x 2 light gray plate with a ball
1—1 x 2 light gray plate with two clips
on the side
1—1 x 2 light gray plate with a handle
on the side
2—2 x 4 light gray tiles

2—light gray plate, modified with pin
hole
2—light gray connector pins
2—large wheels

LAKE
1—blue baseplate
Various tan bricks for the shoreline
1—4 x 6 brown plate for the dock
2—1 x 1 brown round bricks for the dock
Gray bricks for the rocks
Trees and flowers

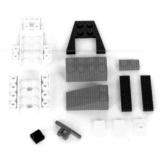

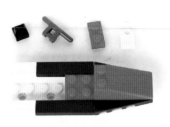

STEP 1: Gather the bricks shown for building the Jet Ski.

STEP 2: Attach the dark blue bricks to the white inverted slope and white inverted wedge as shown.

STEP 3: Place a 2 x 4 red brick in the Jet Ski, and then add the 2 x 4 red slope. Add the two 1 x 2 white tiles to the back of the Jet Ski.

STEP 4: Place the 1 x 2 red plate right behind the 2 x 4 red slope. Then add the 1 x 2 white plate with one stud on top, the black 1 x 1 plate with a clip on top and the handlebars.

STEP 5: Build the trailer! Find two large wheels, a 2 x 4 light gray plate, two 2 x 2 light gray plates with a pin hole and two light gray pins.

STEP 6: Attach the 2 x 2 plates to the wheels using the connector pins. Then attach the 2 x 4 plate between the wheels.

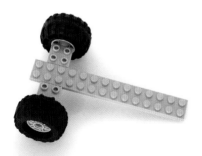

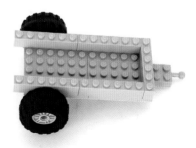

STEP 7: Add a 2 x 14 plate so that it hangs off the wheels by one stud in the back. Or use shorter plates attached together to create the same length.

STEP 8: Place two 6 x 6 plates and a 2 x 2 plate with a ball on the side on top of the 2 x 14 plate.

STEP 9: Build up the sides of the trailer with five 1 x 6 bricks.

STEP 10: Gather the bricks shown for building a ramp on the back of the trailer.

STEP 11: Attach the two 2 x 4 tiles to the 2 x 3 plate and the 1 x 2 plate with two clips on the side. Connect the 1 x 2 plate with a handle on the side to the plate with two clips. Then attach the plate with a handle to the underside of the trailer.

Your minifigures are now ready to load up the car for a day in the sun! Don't forget to pack the camp chairs (page 125) for relaxing on the shore.

Create a LEGO lake with a blue baseplate. Use tan bricks for the shoreline, and add trees and flowers. Build a dock with a 4 x 6 brown plate and two 1 x 1 brown round bricks.

Use gray bricks to build rocks sticking up out of the water. Who will hit the rocks and go flying?

BEARS IN THE TENT

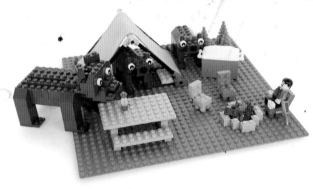

"It's okay, honey," Mom said. "You rest here while I take the kids on a bike ride. We'll try to fit in a little more fun on this trip!"

"Fun?" said Dad. "What fun? We haven't had any fun YET!"

Dad was just starting to relax and enjoy the peaceful sounds of the forest and the afternoon sun glinting through the trees when he noticed a snuffling and crackling sound. "What kind of creature could that be?" he wondered. He didn't have to wonder long because the nose of a little bear cub poked its way out of the tent! And of course its mother and sibling were close behind.

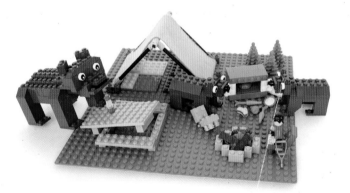

What a time to be laid up with a broken leg! Dad sat there helplessly as the bears tried out the sleeping bags, helped themselves to the contents of the family's cooler, and destroyed the picnic table. They would have ruined the camp chairs as well if it weren't for the sounds of Mom and the kids coming back from their bike ride.

The bears trundled off into the woods as Mom and the kids came back to the camp.

"What have you been doing?" yelled Mom. "This place is a disaster!"

"Don't look at me," Dad said. "It was bears! A mother and her two cubs. They destroyed everything and all I could do was to sit here and watch!"

"Let's just go home," Mom sighed. "I don't think things could get much worse. I'll pack up the tent. We'll just get you home for some rest. Wow, what a terrible vacation!"

BEARS

Make your minifigure family's camping vacation a little more exciting by building a mother bear and her cubs. Once they are complete, build the bears a LEGO stream to catch fish in, or pretend that they are exploring the campground and sampling the food from people's coolers! They might be a nuisance, but thankfully these bears are also adorable!

PARTS LIST
MOTHER BEAR
BROWN BRICKS
2—2 x 8 plates
3—4 x 4 plates
5—2 x 6 plates
5—2 x 4 plates
4—2 x 3 plates
4—1 x 4 plates
9—1 x 2 plates
1—2 x 2 plate
2—2 x 6 bricks
3—2 x 4 bricks
12—2 x 2 bricks
10—1 x 2 bricks
9—1 x 4 bricks

4—2 x 2 slopes
2—1 x 1 bricks
2—1 x 1 bricks with a stud on the side
2—1 x 1 round plates
2—1 x 1 slopes, 30 degree

ASSORTED BRICKS
1—2 x 2 black plate
2—eyes

BEAR CUB
BROWN BRICKS
1—4 x 6 plate
1—2 x 6 plate
1—2 x 3 plate
1—1 x 4 plate
2—1 x 3 plates

4—1 x 2 plates
8—1 x 2 bricks
2—2 x 4 slopes
2—1 x 2 slopes
2—1 x 2 slopes, inverted
2—1 x 1 bricks with a stud on the side
2—1 x 1 bricks with a stud on the side (headlight)
1—1 x 2 plate with one stud on top
2—1 x 1 slopes, 30 degree
2—1 x 1 round plates

ASSORTED BRICKS
1—1 x 1 black round plate
2—eyes

STEP 1: Start with the mother bear's body. Grab a 2 x 6 brown plate and a 1 x 2 brown plate.

STEP 2: Add two 2 x 4 plates.

STEP 3: Place two 2 x 6 plates on top. The plate on the right should hang off by 3 studs and the left plate should hang off by 1 stud.

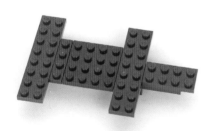

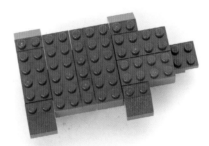

STEP 4: From left to right, add a 2 x 8 plate, a 1 x 4 plate, a 4 x 4 plate, a 2 x 8 plate and a 2 x 4 plate. The longer plates will hold the legs.

STEP 5: Add a layer of brown bricks to the bear's body. Use a 2 x 2 slope on each of the corners where the legs will go.

STEP 6: Gather the bricks shown for building the bear's face.

STEP 7: Stack a 1 x 2 plate on top of a 1 x 4 plate and attach this to two 1 x 2 bricks as shown.

STEP 8: Stack three bricks: a 1 x 4 brown plate, a 2 x 2 black plate and a 1 x 2 brown plate. Then attach this to the bricks from step 7.

STEP 9: Turn the head around and attach the 2 x 2 brown plate to the underside of the black plate.

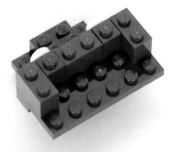

STEP 10: Add two 1 x 2 bricks behind the nose and two 1 x 2 plates on each side of the head.

STEP 11: Add three 1 x 2 bricks and two 1 x 1 bricks with a stud on the side to the head. Add the eyes.

STEP 12: Turn the head around and attach a 2 x 6 plate to the underside of the 1 x 2 bricks from step 11.

STEP 13: Add a 1 x 4 brick behind the eyes. Then place a 2 x 4 plate on top of the head. Add a 1 x 4 plate and a 1 x 2 plate on top of that. Place 1 x 1 slopes on the sides of the head.

STEP 14: Add a 1 x 4 brick on the back of the head. Place two 1 x 1 round plates and a 1 x 2 plate on top.

STEP 15: Place two 1 x 2 bricks on top of the round plates from step 14. Angle them slightly to make them look like ears.

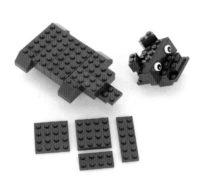

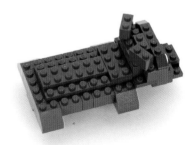

STEP 16: Get ready to connect the parts. Gather the body, head, two 4 x 4 plates, one 2 x 4 plate and one 2 x 6 plate.

STEP 17: Attach the head as shown.

STEP 18: Use the brown plates to make the bear's back more rounded.

STEP 19: Turn the bear upside down. Find six 1 x 4 bricks and two 1 x 1 bricks to add to the belly.

STEP 20: Add the bricks to the underside of the bear as shown.

STEP 21: Build the bear's legs and add them to the body. Each leg is three 2 x 2 bricks and one 2 x 3 plate.

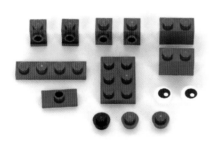

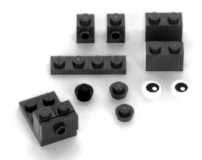

STEP 22: Now build a bear cub! Gather the bricks shown for the head.

STEP 23: Place two 1 x 1 bricks (headlight) on top of a 2 x 3 plate. Then add a 1 x 2 plate with one stud on top.

STEP 24: Add a 1 x 4 plate and a 1 x 1 black round plate for the nose.

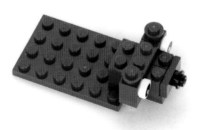

STEP 25: Place two 1 x 1 bricks with a stud on the side, two eyes, one 1 x 2 brick and two 1 x 1 round plates on top of the 1 x 4 plate. The round plates are the ears. Add another 1 x 2 brick to the back of the head.

STEP 26: Attach the head to a 4 x 6 plate.

STEP 27: Add two 2 x 4 slopes, two 1 x 2 slopes and two 1 x 1 slopes to the bear's body.

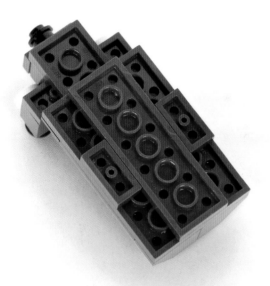

STEP 28: Turn the bear upside down and add a 2 x 6 plate and two 1 x 2 plates.

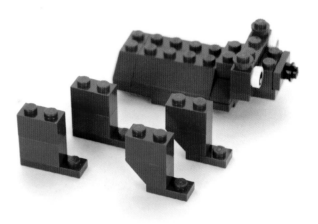

STEP 29: Build the legs. The back legs each have two 1 x 2 bricks and a 1 x 3 plate. The front legs each have a 1 x 2 brick, a 1 x 2 inverted slope and a 1 x 2 plate.

STEP 30: Attach the legs to the body, and the bear cub is complete! Build a second cub to complete the bear family.

Now your bears are ready to get into some mischief!

ONE YEAR LATER . . .

"Remember last year, Dad?" said Addie as the family settled in for some s'mores on their annual camping vacation. "That was the WORST camping trip ever!"

"Yes it was," said Dad. "Don't worry, kids, this year is going to be much better! Listen to the peace and quiet of the woods! We're going to have a great time this year, I can tell."

"I agree," said Mom. "Nothing is going to go wrong this year! It's going to be our best camping vacation ever . . ."

DR. MARTIN'S MUTANT BUG LAB

Build a scientific laboratory where an experiment gone wrong mutates ordinary bugs into terrifying gigantic beasts! A simple scorpion becomes an enormous creature who can lift humans with one claw and a harmless spider becomes a large, hairy threat to public safety! How will the scientists ever get the creatures back to normal size again? Build their adventure with a shrinking machine (that does nothing of the sort), an overconfident animal control officer and his animal catching truck and a robot bug with a shrink blaster gun that finally does the trick.

THE WEIRDEST SUMMER OF MY LIFE

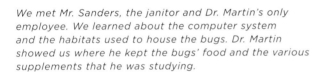

It was summer. Five years ago. The weirdest summer of my life. They say that writing down your thoughts about traumatic experiences can help you deal with them. I guess that's what I'm doing here, although I don't know how anything could help a person get over the nightmare that was my experience that summer. My name is Cliff. Cliff Robertson. I was studying biology at Green Mountain University, and as part of my research project on insects and arachnids, I took an internship at Dr. Martin's research laboratory in the city. Amelia was accepted into the internship as well. We both remember that first day like it was yesterday . . .

We walked into the lab. Everything seemed normal.

"Hello," said Dr. Martin. "Welcome to my laboratory. The main focus of this lab is to find ways to make bugs resilient to the types of chemicals they might encounter out in nature. You know, the bug population has a huge effect on the rest of our valuable ecosystem!"

Yes, Amelia and I both knew that. So far so good.

We met Mr. Sanders, the janitor and Dr. Martin's only employee. We learned about the computer system and the habitats used to house the bugs. Dr. Martin showed us where he kept the bugs' food and the various supplements that he was studying.

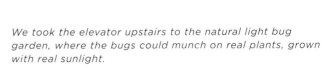

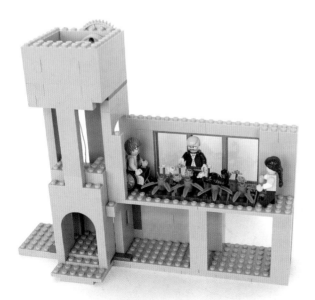

We took the elevator upstairs to the natural light bug garden, where the bugs could munch on real plants, grown with real sunlight.

And then we got the news we weren't expecting. "I'll be heading out now," said Dr. Martin. "I'll be attending a conference for the next two weeks on the migratory patterns of butterflies. While I'm gone, I'd like for you two to work on perfecting a vitamin-infused growth serum that can be given to bugs of all types. It would be so helpful if one serum could help many different species. I'll be expecting great results when I arrive back in two weeks."

And just like that, he was gone!

Amelia and I really had no idea where to begin. We knew all kinds of facts about bugs, but inventing a new growth serum? That sounded impossible. Amelia grabbed a pan and started mixing vitamins together while I scrolled through the Internet, not quite sure what I was looking for.

Unfortunately, Amelia's first attempt was a total disaster. Bright green goo bubbled over the edge of the pan and onto the floor!

We worked together on a different concoction. We added vitamin B6 and zinc and protein powder and several other things that I'm not sure what they were. It looked okay, but would it do anything to make the bugs stronger and healthier?

There was only one way to find out! We decided to go ahead and give the bugs a dose. Amelia carefully poured a little of the serum into each bug habitat.

And then, WOW! We were not expecting results that quickly! Instantly, Dr. Martin's Black Forest scorpion began growing—a LOT!

Amelia and I jumped back in horror as the scorpion turned into a gigantic and threatening mutant scorpion! "RUN!" I yelled to Amelia as I wheeled away behind the stove.

Before we even had time to think, the ugliest, hairiest, most disgusting brown spider was crawling its way out of the habitat next to the scorpion. It was our worst nightmare! Amelia hid under the desk while I just sat there, paralyzed with fright.

BUG RESEARCH LABORATORY

Assemble a science lab with bubbling concoctions and ordinary bugs that become gigantic beasts! This lab is well equipped with a computer station, habitats for the bugs, a storage cabinet, a stove and even a working elevator. Once you have put everything together, dream up some crazy adventures for the poor scientists to get into!

PARTS LIST

BUG HABITATS
2—4 x 10 plates
2—6 x 6 plates
2—2 x 6 plates
4—2 x 4 plates
1—1 x 4 plate
2—1 x 2 plates
8—2 x 4 bricks
1—2 x 6 brick
4—1 x 4 bricks
1—2 x 2 brick
1—2 x 3 x 2 container with door
12—1 x 1 bricks
2—1 x 2—2 x 2 brackets
2—1 x 2 bricks
1—2 x 4 tile
4—1 x 2 x 1 panels
10—1 x 2 x 3 clear panels
Bugs

COMPUTER TABLE
1—4 x 10 dark gray plate
1—4 x 6 dark gray plate
1—1 x 2—1 x 2 dark gray hinge plate
4—1 x 4 dark gray bricks
2—1 x 2 dark gray bricks
1—2 x 2 white slope with a computer screen
2—2 x 4 light gray tiles
1—4 x 4 black plate
1—2 x 2 hinge plate and 1 x 2 hinge base
1 x 2 tiles with screens and buttons
1—chair
1—2 x 2 brick

CABINET
1—2 x 6 dark gray plate
1—2 x 6 light gray plate
6—2 x 3 x 2 containers with translucent doors
Various 1 x 1 dark gray round tiles plus round bricks and cones for building bottles

STOVE
1—4 x 6 dark gray plate
1—1 x 4 dark gray brick with four studs on the side
2—1 x 6 dark gray bricks
2—1 x 2 dark gray bricks
3—1 x 4 dark gray bricks
1—2 x 2 black round plate
1—2 x 2 red round plate
1—pan
1 x 1 round plates for knobs

ELEVATOR
Various light gray bricks and plates
3—1 x 4 windows, 5 bricks high
1—Technic gear, 40 tooth
3—Technic wedge belt wheels
3—blue Technic pins, 3 studs long
1—light gray axle, 6 studs long
1—2 x 2 black tile with a lifting ring
String
Various brown plates and flowers for the garden

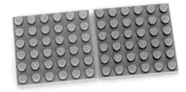

STEP 1: Build some bug habitats! Start with two 6 x 6 plates.

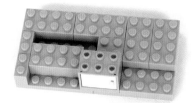

STEP 2: Place the 2 x 3 x 2 container in the front, with a 2 x 4 plate right next to it. Then add five 2 x 4 bricks, a 2 x 2 brick and two 1 x 2 bricks.

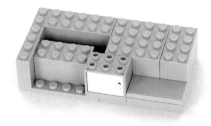

STEP 3: Add another layer of bricks. Place two 2 x 4 plates on top of the brick to the left of the container. Add a 2 x 4 tile on the right side.

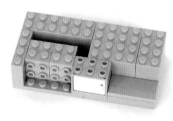

STEP 4: Place two 1 x 2—2 x 2 brackets and two 1 x 2 plates on top of the plates from the previous step.

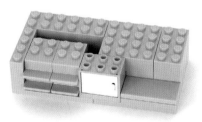

STEP 5: Create shelves by attaching four 1 x 2 x 1 panels to the brackets.

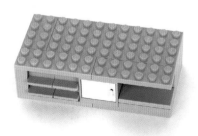

STEP 6: Cover the habitat table with light gray plates.

STEP 7: Use 1 x 2 x 3 clear panels to create the glass for the bug habitat. There are three 1 x 1 light gray bricks stacked on each corner and three 1 x 4 bricks between the two sections of the habitat. Use a 4 x 10 plate and a 1 x 4 plate for the lid on top.

STEP 8: Add some bugs, and your bug habitat is complete!

STEP 9: Build a cabinet for storing bottles and other supplies. Use six 2 x 3 x 2 containers with a 2 x 6 plate on both the top and the bottom. Round bricks and cone bricks in translucent colors make great bottles! Use gray round tiles on the tops of the bricks as lids.

STEP 10: Build a stove top for creating scientific concoctions. Use a 1 x 4 brick with four studs on the side to hold round plates as knobs. For burners, use 2 x 2 round plates. Use a red plate for a burner that is turned on and a black plate for a burner that is off. Use translucent yellow round plates as spilled liquid.

STEP 11: Create a computer workspace with room for two scientists.

STEP 12: Use a 1 x 2—1 x 2 hinge plate to attach two dark gray plates. Add the table legs. Then add computer screens and tiles decorated with buttons and gauges. Build a large computer screen by attaching two 2 x 4 tiles to a 4 x 4 black plate. Then attach this to a hinge brick.

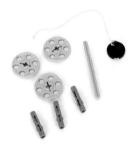

STEP 13: Gather the bricks shown for building the mechanism for the working elevator.

STEP 14: Attach the three Technic pins to two Technic wedge belt wheels stacked together.

STEP 15: Insert the Technic axle and add the other wheel. Tie a knot in a piece of string and thread it through one of the grooves on the blue pin. The knot will keep the string in place. Then tie the other end of the string to the black tile with a ring. Build the elevator car as shown.

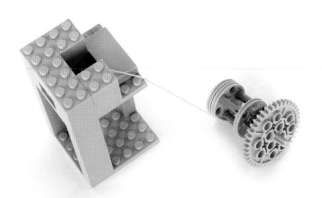

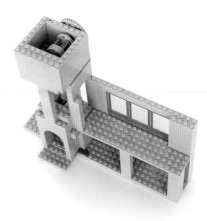

STEP 16: Attach the black tile with the ring to the top of the elevator car. Add a gear to the end of the axle. The gear will provide a handle to turn to operate the elevator.

STEP 17: Remove the large gear, insert the axle through a 1 x 2 Technic brick with a hole, and then replace the large gear. Add this mechanism to the top of the elevator shaft. Turn the large gear, and the string will wind around the blue Technic pins and lift the elevator car! If you don't have the exact bricks shown, adapt this design with what you have.

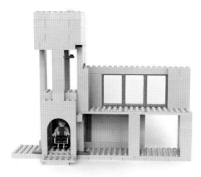

A minifigure can be loaded at the bottom . . .

And then lifted to the second floor! If you want the elevator car to stay at the second floor, use a 2 x 2 plate to temporarily attach it to the second floor. Place two studs of the 2 x 2 plate on the elevator car and the other two on the second floor. Remove it when you're ready for the car to go down again.

Use brown plates and flowers and plants to create a sunlit bug garden on the second floor. Or use the second floor for more scientific equipment.

MUTANT SCORPION

Cliff and Amelia's bug growth serum transformed a tiny ordinary scorpion into this enormous mutant version capable of lifting humans and dismantling a truck! Yikes! Bend his legs and claws into all kinds of crazy positions. What trouble will he get into in your LEGO world?

PARTS LIST

BLACK BRICKS
2—2 x 4 plates
2—2 x 2 plates
8—1 x 2 plates
4—1 x 2 hinge plates with one finger, locking
4—1 x 2 hinge plates with two fingers, locking
2—1 x 2 plates with a handle on the end
2—1 x 2 plates with a handle on the side
2—1 x 4 curved slopes
1—2 x 4 curved slope
1—2 x 2 plate with one stud on top
1—1 x 2 plate with two clips on the side

2—arm mechanical
1—2 x 3 x ⅔ modified brick with wing end, two studs

GRAY BRICKS
1—1 x 2 x ⅔ light gray modified brick with studs on the sides
1—1 x 2 light gray brick
6—1 x 2 light gray plates with a socket on the side
1—1 x 2 light gray plate with two clips on the side
2—1 x 1 light gray plates
1—antenna
2—1 x 2 dark gray plates with a handle on the end
4—1 x 2 dark gray plates with a ball and a socket

4—1 x 2 dark gray plates with a ball on the side
2—1 x 2 dark gray plates with a ball on the end
1—1 x 2 dark gray plate with one stud on top
4—1 x 1 dark gray round plates
2—silver arm mechanical
4—silver barbs

ASSORTED BRICKS
2—2 x 2 orange domes
2—2 x 4 yellow plates
1—2 x 3 yellow plate
1—2 x 2 translucent black curved slope with lip

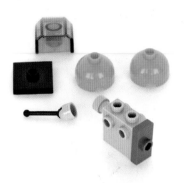

STEP 1: Gather the bricks shown for building the scorpion's head.

STEP 2: Attach the modified brick with studs on the side to a 1 x 2 light gray brick. Attach the 1 x 2 plate with one stud on top to the end.

STEP 3: Finish building the head as shown. Attach the head to a 2 x 2 black plate with one stud on top.

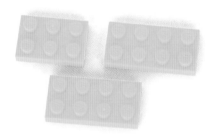

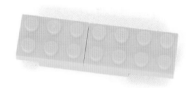

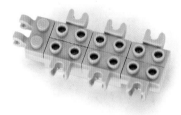

STEP 4: Grab two 2 x 4 yellow plates and a 2 x 3 yellow plate for building the scorpion's body.

STEP 5: Stack the plates as shown.

STEP 6: Add six 1 x 2 plates with a socket on the side and one 1 x 2 plate with two clips.

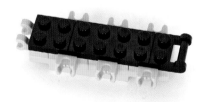

STEP 7: Attach a 2 x 2 black plate, a 2 x 4 black plate and a 1 x 2 black plate with a handle on the side.

STEP 8: Place a 2 x 4 black plate at the end with the black handle. Then add two 1 x 2 black plates.

STEP 9: Attach a 2 x 4 curved slope and a 2 x 3 x ⅔ modified brick with wing end. Then gather the bricks shown for building the tail.

STEP 10: Assemble the tail as shown.

STEP 11: Attach the tail to the scorpion's body. Use a 1 x 2 plate with two clips on the side to attach the head to the other end of the body.

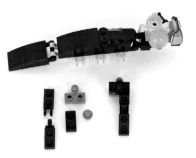

STEP 12: Assemble two back legs as shown.

STEP 13: Build two middle legs as shown.

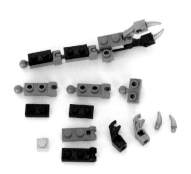

STEP 14: Gather the bricks shown for the two front claws. Get creative with the bricks you have if you don't have the exact pieces shown.

STEP 15: Connect two 1 x 2 plates with a ball on one end and a socket on the other end. Add a 1 x 2 plate with a ball on the side and two 1 x 2 black plates.

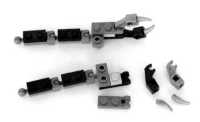

STEP 16: Add a 1 x 2 black plate with a handle on the end and a 1 x 1 light gray plate. Place a 1 x 1 round plate under the plate with a ball on the side and next to the black plate with a handle on the end.

STEP 17: Complete the claw arms as shown. Build the claws as mirror images of each other.

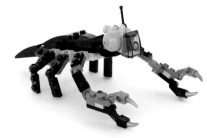

STEP 18: Attach the claw arms, and the scorpion is complete! Now pretend that he is grabbing minifigures, lifting furniture or taking apart a car! There is no telling what this crazy bug will do.

GIGANTIC CRAWLING SPIDER

Construct a giant creepy crawly spider! It's a good thing this enormous spider is not real. Give him black beady eyes, fangs and posable legs so that you can pretend that he is creeping and crawling on everything imaginable!

PARTS LIST

BROWN BRICKS

4—2 x 4 plates
2—1 x 3 plates
12—1 x 2 plates
2—1 x 2 curved slopes
6—1 x 2 hinge plates with two fingers
4—1 x 2 slopes
1—2 x 4 wedge, triple right
1—2 x 4 wedge, triple left

BLACK BRICKS

1—2 x 6 plate
1—2 x 3 plate
1—1 x 2 plate
2—1 x 1 round plates
6—1 x 2 plates with a clip on the end
6—1 x 2 hinge plates with one finger
2—1 x 2 plates with angled handles on the side

ASSORTED BRICKS

2—1 x 1 white plate with one vertical tooth
2—1 x 2 light gray plates with a socket on the end
2—1 x 2 dark gray plates with a ball on the side
2—1 x 2 dark gray plates with a socket and a ball

STEP 1: Start the spider's body with a 2 x 4 plate.

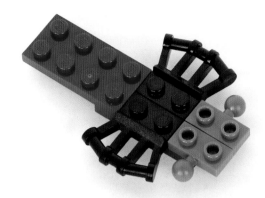

STEP 2: Add two 1 x 2 plates with a ball on the side, two 1 x 2 plates with angled bars and another 2 x 4 brown plate.

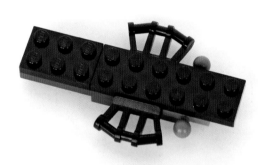

STEP 3: Add a 2 x 6 black plate and a 2 x 3 black plate.

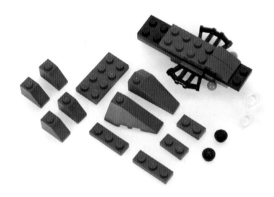

STEP 4: Place a 1 x 2 black plate on the third row of studs from the right. Then add two 1 x 2 curved slopes and a 2 x 4 plate. Gather the bricks shown.

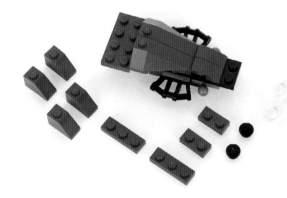

STEP 5: Add the two 2 x 4 wedge bricks and the 2 x 4 plate.

STEP 6: Complete the back of the body with four 1 x 2 slopes and add 1 x 1 round plates for eyes.

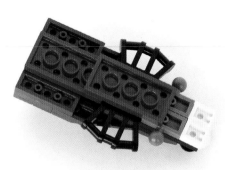

STEP 7: Add the two 1 x 2 plates to the underside of the body, and then add the two 1 x 3 plates.

STEP 8: Build two front legs using a 1 x 2 plate with a socket, a 1 x 2 plate with a ball and a socket and two 1 x 2 brown plates each.

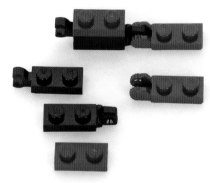

STEP 9: Build 6 back legs. For each use a 1 x 2 black plate with a clip, a 1 x 2 black hinge plate with one finger, a 1 x 2 brown hinge plate with two fingers and a 1 x 2 brown plate.

STEP 10: Attach all the legs, and the spider is complete!

Now your spider is ready to get into trouble! Create a scene with the spider emptying out the cabinets in the bug lab. Or pretend that he is overturning cars or climbing the side of a building. So many fun possibilities with a spider this size!

EXTREME ANIMAL CONTROL!

Neither Amelia nor I had any idea what we should do with these awful gigantic bugs! Obviously, a fly swatter was going to be no match for these guys. So we did the first thing that came to mind. We opened the large back door and let them escape. Twenty seconds later, we realized that that was probably not the smartest idea considering that there was a park next door.

We rushed out to the park, but by the time we arrived the bugs were already wreaking havoc on the equipment and the people enjoying the beautiful day!

"What's that green flying thing?" I asked Amelia.

"I don't know!" she responded. "That serum somehow made its way to every bug in the building! It's like a mutated butterfly or something! A venomous butterfly—with CLAWS!"

"Can we call animal control?" I asked.

"I'm already looking up the number," said Amelia. "Oh, here's a guy called 'Brawny Bob, the Extreme Animal Control Guy.' That sounds good! I'll call him."

Brawny Bob showed up quickly with his truck. "What can I help you with?" he asked.

"Uh," I stammered. "We've had a little accident with some bugs. They mutated to many times their original size. Can you handle them?"

"No beast is too strong for me," bragged Bob. "Where are they?"

"Oh, you can't miss them!" I said.

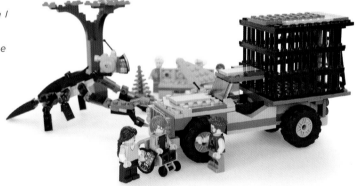

Bob got right to work trying to wrangle the giant bugs. He ejected a rope from his grappling gun and quickly had the venomous butterfly all tied up.

But it looked like that awful scorpion was going to have the last laugh!

"Don't worry, everyone," said Bob. "I've still got everything under control!"

Brawny Bob managed to get free from the grip of the scorpion's awful claws, and he loaded up the winged bug into his truck. The scorpion ran off unscathed, and the giant spider was nowhere to be found. Still, one for three was better than having captured none at all! "Where do you want me to take this thing?" asked Brawny Bob.

"I don't know," I answered. "Somewhere away from here! I thought you guys took animals to the shelter or something."

"This thing? There's no way anyone will want to adopt this, even if I could talk the shelter into taking it!" said Bob.

So in the end, Bob dropped the butterfly off at the lab, and we were right back where we started.

By the time we got back to the lab, Mr. Sanders, the janitor, had fixed the bug habitats. Little good that would do us since these bugs could only fit one of their gigantic hairy feet inside, but we appreciated his efforts. The pesky venomous butterfly perched on top of the bug habitats, and some strange green beetle with hideous bulging eyes was crawling all over the computer desk. My skin was crawling right along with it!

EXTREME ANIMAL CONTROL TRUCK

This truck is not just your everyday animal control truck. This truck is for animals of extreme size! It's a good thing that the truck driver is calm and confident because he is going to deal with some really weird creatures!

PARTS LIST

DARK GRAY BRICKS
1—6 x 8 plate
2—4 x 8 plates
1—4 x 6 plate
1—2 x 12 plate
3—4 x 4 plates
5—2 x 6 plates
3—2 x 4 plates
2—2 x 3 plates
2—2 x 2 plates
3—1 x 6 plates
5—1 x 4 plates
5—1 x 2 plates
2—1 x 6 tiles
2—1 x 4 tiles
1—2 x 4 brick
1—2 x 2 brick
4—1 x 2 slopes, inverted
2—2 x 4 plates with two pins
4—1 x 2 grills

LIGHT GRAY BRICKS
2—6 x 6 plates
1—4 x 4 plate
1—2 x 4 plate
2—1 x 4 plates
1—2 x 2 plate
2—1 x 3 plates
2—1 x 2 plates
1—2 x 3 wedge plate, right
1—2 x 3 wedge plate, left
2—2 x 4 tiles
2—1 x 6 tiles
2—1 x 4 tiles
4—1 x 3 slopes
2—1 x 4 bricks
3—1 x 6 bricks
2—1 x 4 Technic bricks
2—1 x 1 slopes, 30 degree
4—1 x 2 x 1 ⅓ bricks with a curved top
1—1 x 2 plate with a handle on the side, free ends

BLACK BRICKS
1—6 x 8 plate
2—2 x 8 plates
1—2 x 4 plate
2—1 x 4 x 1 panels
1—1 x 2 brick
1—1 x 2 brick, five bricks high
1—1 x 4 brick, four studs on the side
1—1 x 2—1 x 4 bracket
2—1 x 2 plates
1—ladder with clips
18—1 x 4 x 2 spindled fences with two studs
1—door with bars

ASSORTED BRICKS
4—large wheels
1—2 x 4 translucent black windshield, two bricks high
1—steering wheel
4—blue connector pins, ½ length
1—1 x 2 white tile
2—1 x 2 dark red tiles
2—1 x 2 translucent yellow plates
4—1 x 1 translucent red round tiles

STEP 1: Line up a 2 x 2 plate, a 2 x 12 plate and a 2 x 3 plate as shown.

STEP 2: Add a 1 x 4 plate, a 2 x 4 plate with two pins, a 2 x 4 plate, a 6 x 6 plate, a 2 x 2 plate, another 2 x 4 plate with two pins and a 1 x 2—1 x 4 bracket.

STEP 3: Add another layer of plates, leaving an opening for the driver to sit. From left to right, add three 2 x 4 plates, two 2 x 6 plates, a 2 x 3 plate and a 2 x 4 plate.

STEP 4: Place a 4 x 4 dark gray plate over the first stud on the right end of each 2 x 6 plate from the previous step. Add a 2 x 2 light gray plate in front of that. Then add a layer of bricks as shown. Place two 1 x 2 dark gray plates on top of the Technic brick.

STEP 5: Add a 1 x 6 dark gray plate and two 1 x 3 light gray slopes to each side of the cab. Add a 1 x 4 plate and a 2 x 4 plate on the back of the truck. Then stack a 1 x 4 dark gray plate on top of a 1 x 4 light gray plate. Add a 1 x 4 x 1 black panel on top. Make two of these.

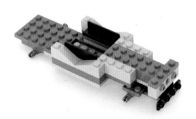

STEP 6: Place one panel unit on each side of the cab. Insert the blue connector pins into the Technic brick as shown.

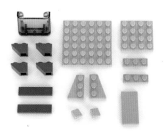

STEP 7: Gather the bricks shown for building the hood of the truck.

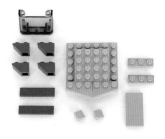

STEP 8: Place the 4 x 4 plate and the two 2 x 3 wedge plates on top of the 6 x 6 plate.

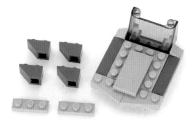

STEP 9: Add the tiles, windshield and 1 x 1 slopes.

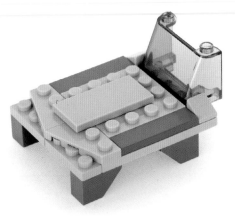

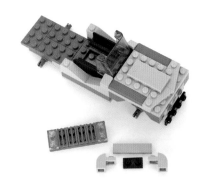

STEP 10: Place the two 1 x 3 wedge plates under the front of the hood, and then add the four 1 x 2 inverted slopes. The inverted slopes will hold the 1 x 3 plates in place.

STEP 11: Attach the hood. Then build the front grill and the front bumper as shown. Attach the 1 x 2 black plate and the two curved top bricks to the 1 x 4 tile.

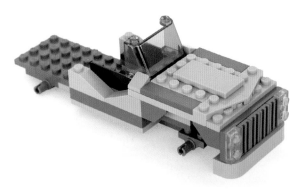

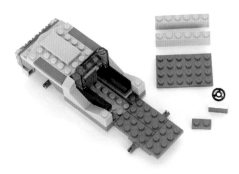

STEP 12: Place the grill and the bumper on the front of the truck.

STEP 13: Stack two 1 x 2 dark gray plates and place them under the steering wheel. Then gather the bricks shown.

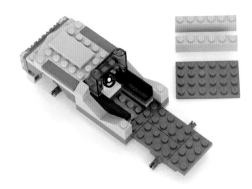

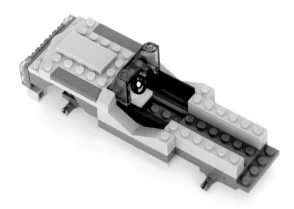

STEP 14: Place the 1 x 2 dark gray plate just behind where the driver will sit.

STEP 15: Attach the 4 x 6 plate and the two 1 x 6 bricks to the back of the truck.

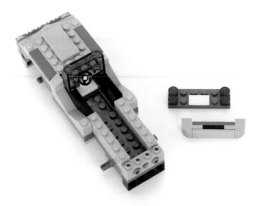

STEP 16: Build the rear end of the truck. Insert two blue pins (½ length) into a Technic brick and attach across the back. Place a 1 x 4 black brick with four studs on the side under the back end of the truck. Then build the back bumper and the taillights.

STEP 17: Place the bumper and taillights on the truck. Then add a 1 x 6 plate, two 1 x 2 light gray plates, a 1 x 4 plate and a 2 x 6 plate. Gather the bricks shown.

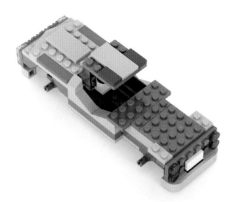

STEP 18: Add the 4 x 4 plate and the roof of the cab.

STEP 19: Get creative with a bug cage for the back of the truck. The cage shown has a base built from a 6 x 8 plate and a 4 x 8 plate. Use a ladder with two clips and a 1 x 2 plate with a handle on the end to add a ladder to the back of the truck.

STEP 20: Add the wheels, bug cage and ladder, and the truck is complete!

Brawny Bob is working so hard to contain the bugs, but the bugs are more than he bargained for! Pretend that Bob is catching one bug, while another one takes apart his truck! Or pretend that the bugs are flying off with his tools. Poor Bob!

BUG-EYED BEETLE

What's worse than a green beetle? A giant green beetle! This creepy creature has enormous bug eyes, three body sections and legs that bend. Pose your beetle on top of the computer desk, looking down at everyone with his giant eyes. Maybe he'll take a bite right out of the computer screen!

PARTS LIST

LIME GREEN BRICKS
4—2 x 6 plates
4—2 x 4 plates
2—1 x 4 plates
4—1 x 2 plates
1—2 x 3 plate
2—2 x 2 plates
2—1 x 1 plates
1—2 x 3 wedge plate, right

1—2 x 3 wedge plate, left
1—2 x 4 wedge plate
1—2 x 4 brick
4—2 x 2 slopes
2—2 x 2 domes
2—1 x 2 slopes with four slots

DARK GRAY BRICKS
6—1 x 2 hinge plates with one finger, locking
6—1 x 2 hinge plates with two fingers, locking

2—1 x 2 plates with a handle on the end
2—1 x 2 plates with a clip on the end
2—1 x 2 plates with a ball on the side
4—1 x 2 plates with a ball on the end

ASSORTED BRICKS
2—1 x 1 white plates with a vertical tooth
6—1 x 2 light gray plates with a socket on the side

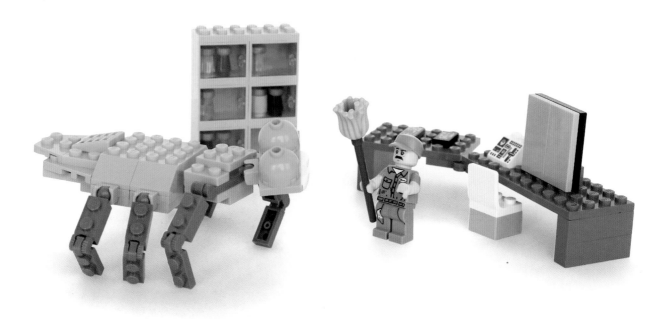

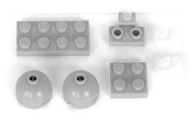

STEP 1: Gather the bricks shown for building the beetle's head.

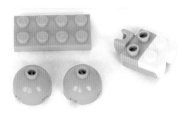

STEP 2: Attach the two 1 x 1 white plates with a tooth and the 1 x 2 light gray plate with a socket on the side to the 2 x 2 plate.

STEP 3: Add the 2 x 4 plate and the 2 x 2 dome bricks as eyes.

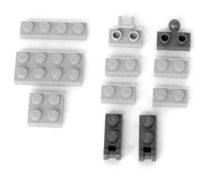

STEP 4: Gather the bricks shown for building the second body segment.

STEP 5: Attach two 1 x 2 dark gray plates with a handle on the end and a 1 x 4 lime green plate to a 2 x 4 lime green plate.

STEP 6: Add a 1 x 2 plate with a ball on the side and three 1 x 2 plates.

STEP 7: Place the 2 x 2 plate on top of this body segment.

STEP 8: Place the 1 x 2 light gray plate with a socket on the side and the last 1 x 2 lime green plate on the underside of this body segment.

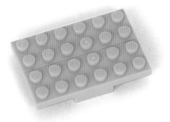

STEP 9: Begin building the third body segment. Attach two 2 x 6 plates to a 2 x 4 plate.

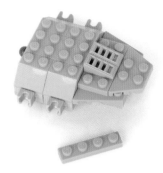

STEP 10: Add two more 2 x 6 plates, four 1 x 2 plates with a socket on the side, a 1 x 2 plate with a ball on the side and two 1 x 1 plates.

STEP 11: Build up the body with a 2 x 4 brick and four 2 x 2 slopes. Then add a 2 x 3 plate and two 2 x 3 wedge plates to the tail end of the body.

STEP 12: Add a 2 x 4 plate, a 2 x 4 wedge plate and two 1 x 2 slopes with four slots. Find a 1 x 4 plate.

STEP 13: Turn the body of the beetle upside down and add the 1 x 4 plate.

STEP 14: Attach the body segments to each other. Build the bug's two front legs. Each leg has a 1 x 2 hinge plate with two fingers, a 1 x 2 hinge plate with one finger and a 1 x 2 plate with a clip on the end.

STEP 15: Assemble four back legs as shown. Each back leg has a 1 x 2 plate with a ball on the end, a 1 x 2 hinge plate with two fingers and a 1 x 2 hinge plate with one finger. If you don't have these exact bricks, get creative with what you have. Substitute plates with clips for the hinge plates if you have those.

STEP 16: Attach all of the legs, and the beetle is complete!

Pretend that your beetle is fighting with the giant scorpion! Or pretend that he is destroying the computer desk in the bug lab or knocking down trees in the park. A beetle this size is a lot of trouble!

THE SHRINKING MACHINE

It was a miserable couple of days after that. Everywhere we turned there were gigantic bugs, and we had no idea how to shrink them back to their original size. Finally, I had an idea. I asked Amelia to shoo all of the bugs outside so that I could work on a machine that just might do the trick. Amelia reluctantly agreed. "But hurry!" she said. "I'm not sure how long I can keep that scorpion from lifting kids right off their bikes at the park!"

I got to work straight away building a machine that would shrink the bugs. If my plan was successful, we would simply stick the bugs inside the machine, run it through a cycle, and the bugs would be tiny again!

When it was complete, I called Mr. Sanders and Amelia. "Let's do this!" I said.

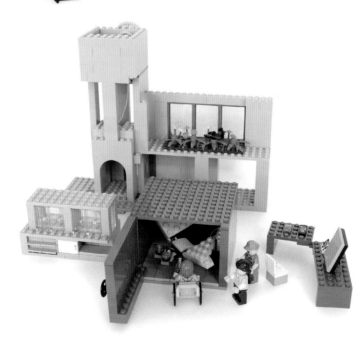

We decided to shrink that awful butterfly with her terrible giant claws first. She was the peskiest bug of the bunch, always buzzing right over our heads and leaving her enormous droppings all over the place. Mr. Sanders had definitely had enough of the constant mopping!

(continued)

Amelia and I stuffed her into the machine, closed the door, programmed the computer and waited. Then, we opened the door . . .

"Yikes!" I screamed. "She's not any smaller!"

"No, she's not," shouted Amelia. "And that's not the only problem. Look!"

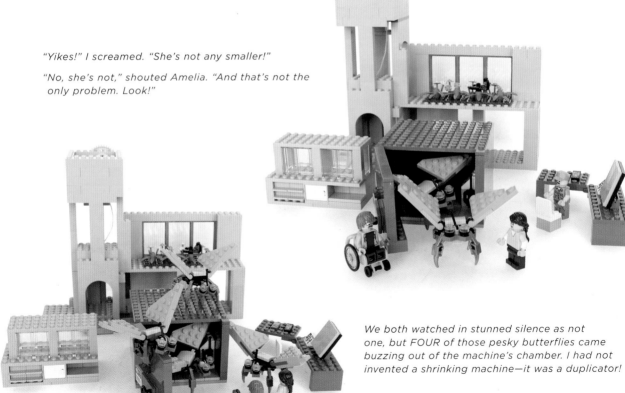

We both watched in stunned silence as not one, but FOUR of those pesky butterflies came buzzing out of the machine's chamber. I had not invented a shrinking machine—it was a duplicator!

VENOMOUS MUTANT BUTTERFLY

This creature is a buttefly gone bad as a result of Cliff and Amelia's not-so-helpful growth serum! Perch her wherever you like by posing her long claws or pretend that she is flying away from a very frustrated Brawny Bob. Build one, or build a whole army to go with the Duplicator Machine (page 181)!

PARTS LIST

- 2—4 x 4 lime green wedge plates
- 1—2 x 3 lime green wedge plate, right
- 1—2 x 3 lime green wedge plate, left
- 2—1 x 4 lime green plates
- 1—2 x 2 black plate modified with an octagonal bar
- 4—gray arms mechanical
- 4—gray barbs
- 2—1 x 1 black plates with a horizontal clip
- 1—1 x 1 dark gray plate with a horizontal clip
- 2—1 x 2 dark gray plates with a handle on the side
- 1—2 x 2 dark gray round plate
- 1—2 x 2 light gray round plate with rounded bottom
- 1—2 x 2 tan curved slope
- 1—2 x 2 green corner plate
- 2—1 x 1 black round plates
- 2—1 x 1 translucent yellow round plates
- 1—antenna

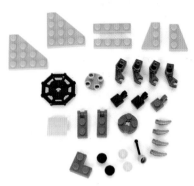

STEP 1: Gather the bricks shown for building the mutant butterfly.

STEP 2: Attach the 2 x 2 light gray round plate to the underside of the black octagonal plate and attach the 2 x 2 dark gray round plate to the top.

STEP 3: Place the two black 1 x 1 plates with a clip on top of the 2 x 2 dark gray round plate. Then add the 2 x 2 tan curved slope. Attach the legs and barbs.

STEP 4: Build the wings. Attach a 2 x 3 wedge plate and a 1 x 2 plate with a handle on the end to a 4 x 4 wedge plate.

STEP 5: Complete both wings as shown.

STEP 6: Build the head. Stack the two 1 x 1 translucent yellow round plates on top of the black round plates. Place these and the antenna on top of the green corner plate. Attach the dark gray 1 x 1 plate with a clip to the body. This will hold the head.

STEP 7: Attach the head, and the mutant butterfly is complete! Then build a few more so that you can pretend the butterflies are being duplicated! Use different colors if you need to—they don't all have to match.

DUPLICATOR MACHINE

Cliff meant to create a machine that would shrink enormous bugs, but ended up creating a duplicator instead! Build along with the story by making your own LEGO duplicator machine. Then pretend that one venomous butterfly is duplicated into a whole army of destructive critters!

PARTS LIST

- 2—6 x 12 green plates, or use plates of any color
- Various dark gray bricks and plates
- Light gray tiles for the floor
- Dark gray tiles for the top of the door
- Dark gray plates for the top of the machine
- 3—1 x 2—2 x 2 brackets for the door handle and buttons
- 1—1 x 2 brick with two studs on the side to hold the red and green lights
- Slope bricks with computer screens
- 1—2 x 2 plate with one stud on top
- 1—Technic steering wheel, 3 stud diameter
- 1—1 x 1 translucent green round plate
- 1—1 x 1 translucent red round plate
- 2—1 x 2—1 x 2 dark gray hinge plates
- Various 1 x 2 tiles with buttons and gauges—use what you have

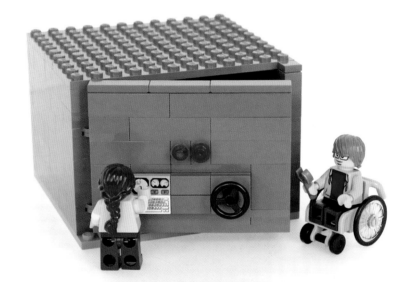

Use two 6 x 12 plates for the base of the machine. The door has three 1 x 2—2 x 2 brackets to hold the tiles with gauges and the steering wheel. The steering wheel is attached to a 2 x 2 plate with one stud on top.

Build the door with two hinges to make it open and close. Use two 1 x 2—1 x 2 hinge plates. Stack two 1 x 2 dark gray plates on top of each side of the hinges to make them the same height as bricks. Add computer screens and other accessories to the machine, and your machine will be ready for action! What will you duplicate first?

AND FINALLY, THEY WERE SMALL AGAIN

After the disastrous results of the shrinking machine, I was determined to find a way to shrink those bugs once and for all! Dr. Martin's return was getting closer every minute, and we certainly did not want him to come back and find this disaster in his lab! I came up with two ideas. Using technology that I saw in a movie, I would invent a shrink blaster gun. But how would I get close enough to those bugs to operate the gun? An insect mech that I could ride on would be just the thing!

I got to work immediately. The insect mech would need to be lightweight and agile, yet sturdy enough to provide protection if one of those crazy bugs attacked me.

I worked all night on the insect mech and the shrink blaster gun. I was so tired that I could hardly hold my eyes open, but I couldn't let another day go by with those enormous bugs terrorizing the lab and, well, the entire block!

When Amelia entered the lab the next morning, I showed her what I had created. "It's a shrink blaster! With this we can shrink those bugs for good."

"But what if they attack you before you can shrink them?" Amelia asked.

"I've thought of that, too," I said. "Meet the GB 64-30 Insect Mech. Those bugs will think it's just another bug and won't even see the shrink blaster coming!"

"I like it!" said Amelia, "But what does GB stand for?"

"For 'great big' of course!" I responded. "It had to be huge to match the size of these awful insects!"

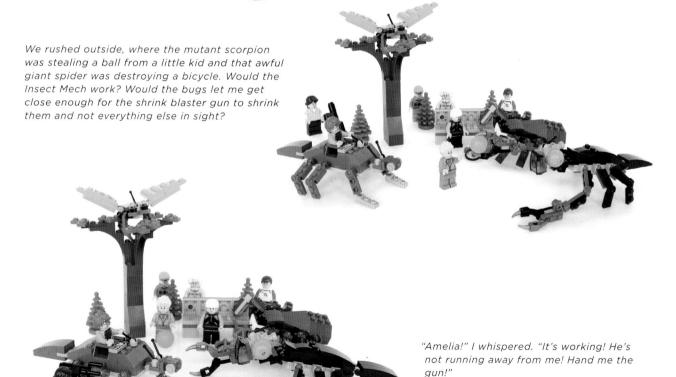

We rushed outside, where the mutant scorpion was stealing a ball from a little kid and that awful giant spider was destroying a bicycle. Would the Insect Mech work? Would the bugs let me get close enough for the shrink blaster gun to shrink them and not everything else in sight?

"Amelia!" I whispered. "It's working! He's not running away from me! Hand me the gun!"

(continued)

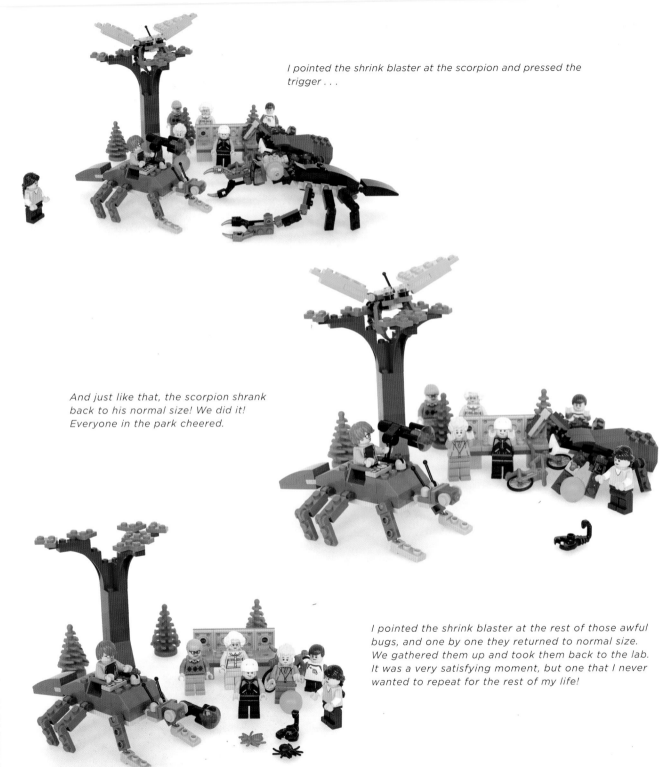

I pointed the shrink blaster at the scorpion and pressed the trigger . . .

And just like that, the scorpion shrank back to his normal size! We did it! Everyone in the park cheered.

I pointed the shrink blaster at the rest of those awful bugs, and one by one they returned to normal size. We gathered them up and took them back to the lab. It was a very satisfying moment, but one that I never wanted to repeat for the rest of my life!

GB 64-30 INSECT MECH

Help Cliff and Amelia shrink the mutant bugs with this insect mech and shrink blaster gun! A minifigure can ride the insect mech and control its actions, allowing it to get close to the real bugs without being eaten. Build your mech with plenty of awesome buttons and controls.

PARTS LIST

DARK GRAY BRICKS
1—4 x 8 plate
1—2 x 4 plate
1—1 x 4 plate
1—2 x 3 plate
4—1 x 2 plates
1—2 x 4 slope
1—3 x 4 slope
1—1 x 4 brick
8—1 x 2 hinge plates with one finger, locking
4—1 x 2 hinge plates with two fingers, locking
1—1 x 2 hinge plate with one finger on the side, locking

2—1 x 2 plates with a ball on the side
1—1 x 2—1 x 2 bracket, inverted
2—1 x 2 plates with a ball and a socket
1—1 x 2 plate with one stud on top
2—1 x 4 curved slopes
1—1 x 1 brick with studs on two sides
2—1 x 2 tiles with handle

LIGHT GRAY BRICKS
1—1 x 2 plate with two clips on the side
1—1 x 2 plate with a handle on the side
1—1 x 2 hinge plate with two fingers on the side, locking
2—1 x 2 plates with a socket on the end
3—antennas

ASSORTED BRICKS
4—1 x 2 brown hinge plates with two fingers, locking
2—1 x 1 lime green round plates
1—1 x 2 tile with gauges
1—1 x 1 translucent red round plate
2—4 x 4 tan plates
1—2 x 4 tan plate

SHRINK BLASTER
1—1 x 1 black round brick
1—black Technic liftarm, 1 x 2 with bar
1—black assembly element, ID 4532220
1—1 x 1 red cone
1—2 x 2 translucent red dish

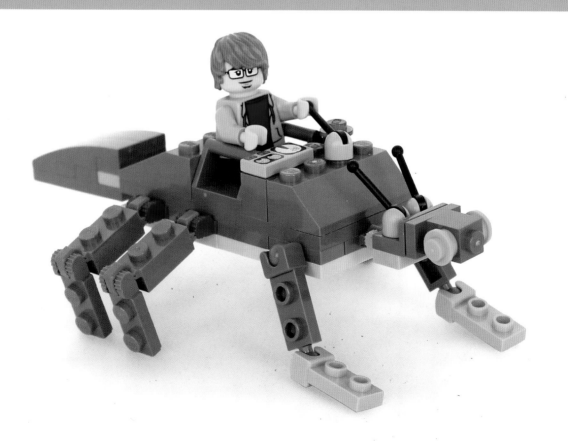

STEP 1: Attach two 4 x 4 tan plates to the top of a 2 x 4 tan plate.

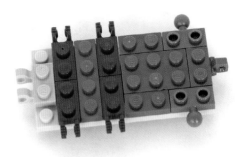

STEP 2: Add the plates shown which will hold the insect mech's legs, head and tail.

STEP 3: Place a 4 x 8 plate on top of the body.

STEP 4: Add a 3 x 4 slope, a 1 x 4 brick and a 2 x 4 slope. Place a 1 x 2 tile with a handle on each side of the cockpit. Then add buttons, gauges and an antenna to the cockpit.

STEP 5: Use 1 x 2 hinge plates and 1 x 2 plates with balls and sockets to create legs for the insect mech.

STEP 6: Gather the bricks shown for building the insect mech's head.

STEP 7: Attach two 1 x 1 lime green round plates to the 1 x 1 brick with studs on two sides. Attach a 1 x 2 plate with one stud on top to a 1 x 2—1 x 2 inverted bracket. Then attach this to a 1 x 2 hinge plate with two fingers on the side.

STEP 8: Place the eyes and the antennas on the insect mech's head as shown.

STEP 9: Gather the bricks shown for building the insect mech's tail.

STEP 10: Attach the 1 x 2 plate to the 2 x 4 plate. Then add the 1 x 2 plate with handle on the side and the other 1 x 2 plate.

STEP 11: Place the two 1 x 4 curved slopes on the tail, and then attach the tail to the body.

STEP 12: Now build the shrink blaster gun! Gather the bricks shown.

STEP 13: Assemble the shrink blaster, and your minifigures will be ready to get rid of those enormous bugs!

Pretend that the giant bugs are shrinking back to normal size! Or pretend that your minifigures have accidentally shrunk the wrong things. This shrink blaster could lead to all kinds of funny adventures!

DR. MARTIN RETURNS

We were just putting the bugs back in their habitats when Dr. Martin came walking in from his conference. Whew! Talk about good timing! "How was everything at the lab while I was gone?" asked Dr. Martin.

"Oh, it was fine," said Amelia.

"Yeah," I agreed. "We worked on the serum, just like you asked us to."

"Well, did you have any success?" asked Dr. Martin.

"No, not much," said Amelia with a sort of vacant expression on her face.

"Is this your concoction here? Let's try it out. I'll go ahead and give some to each of the bugs," said Dr. Martin as he tipped the flask over each habitat.

"WAIT! NOOOOOOO!" I screamed.

And that was the end of our internship, because Amelia and I ran out the door of the lab and never came back.

I decided to finish my degree in accounting, and Amelia became a dentist.

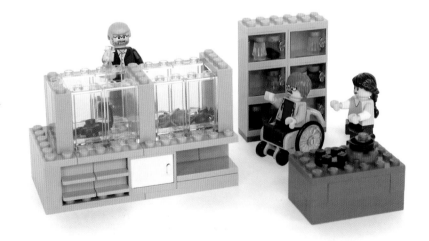

ACKNOWLEDGMENTS

Thank you to everyone at Page Street Publishing for making this LEGO book come to life! I have enjoyed working with every one of you. My editor Sarah did a tremendous job making this book the best it could be!

Many, many thanks to my husband, my parents and Angela Speers for providing childcare so that I could edit photos and write instructions. Thank you to Addie and Scott Spangler for helpful feedback on projects and ideas. Thank you to Micah Sears for inspiring the air traffic control tower. I am so grateful to Rachel Miller, Asia Citro and Dayna Abraham for providing feedback on the book and the book writing process.

My boys created some of the designs in this book. Thank you to Aidan (age 13) for the designs on the alien space cruiser, the biplane, the Jeep, the roadster, the SUV, the Jet Ski, the gigantic crawling spider, the elevator and the bug catcher's truck. Thank you to Gresham (age 10) for the design on the pteranodon, the venomous butterfly and for helping with the other dinosaurs and bugs. Thank you to Owen (age 7) for the design on the space ship. Not every kid gets to say that their LEGO creations are in a book—what a fun adventure this was!

Finally, thank you to all of our loyal Frugal Fun for Boys and Girls readers for your encouragement and support!

ABOUT THE AUTHOR

Sarah Dees is an educator, wife to her wonderful husband Jordan and a busy mom of five LEGO-loving kids. She enjoys learning and exploring the outdoors with her kids, as well as creating all kinds of neat LEGO projects. It's not unusual for her playroom floor to be covered with LEGO bricks—with the whole family building! Her blog, Frugal Fun for Boys and Girls, is packed full of crafts, activities and games that kids will love. Check out her latest projects, including LEGO ideas, at frugalfun4boys.com.

INDEX